Ensemble

An ENSEMBLE co-production ..

A CLOUD IN TROUSERS

By Steve Trafford

First performance of this production:
The Studio, York Theatre Royal,
St Leonard's Place,
York YO1 7HD
Friday 1st October 2004.

The Cast

In order of appearance:

Vladimir Mayakovsky	John Sackville
Lili Brik	Elizabeth Mansfield
Osip Brik	Robert Pickavance
Annushka	Gilly Tompkins

Dramaturg: Elizabeth Mansfield

Director: Damian Cruden
Designer: Simon Banham
Lighting designer: Judith Cloke
Original music & sound design: Christopher Madin
Company stage manager: Shane Thom
Deputy stage manager: Maria Baker
Publicity design: Simon Williams
Marketing manager: Kym Bartlett
Press & publicity: Alex Gammie
Production photographs: Ken Reynolds

*The action of the play takes place in Russia,
in the Soviet Union, between 1915 and 1930*

The play is in two Acts.

*Running time approximately 2 hours,
including one interval.*

Biographies

Simon Banham Designer

Simon has spent the past 20 years designing and devising theatre. His work has been mainly freelance, occasionally associated with particular companies – Head of Design at the 'Contact Theatre', Manchester: 'Quarantine' – performance research company – founder member (1999 – present) and a 20 year relationship with the contemporary chamber opera company 'Music Theatre Wales'.

Recent designs include *Ion* at the Opera National du Rhin in Strasbourg-France, *Don Giovanni* for Opera Vest in Bergen- Norway, *Rantsoen* for Victoria Theatre Company and Quarantine in Gent – Belgium.

His next productions are the premiere of Nigel Osborne's new opera *The Piano Tuner* for Music Theatre Wales and *Butterfly,* a Quarantine project in association with the Tramway Theatre, Glasgow.

He also lectures in Scenography at the University of Wales, Aberystwyth.

Judith Cloke Lighting Designer

Judith Trained at Welsh College of Music & Drama, Cardiff.

After leaving the college she spent a few years at Theatre Royal, Bury St Edmunds, before joining the Electrics Department at York Theatre Royal. She is currently working at the theatre as Chief Electrician.

Her theatre credits at York Theatre Royal include: *The Derby McQueen Affair*;*The Beautiful Thing* and *The Cello And The Nightingale*. *Jesus Christ Superstar* and *Me and My Girl*, for York Light Opera Company; *Peter Grimes* and *Carmen*, for York Opera.

Judith has also overseen the lighting design for a number of productions by the Theatre's Education Department including *The Chrysalids* and *The Selfish Giant.*

Damian Cruden Director

Damian has been Artistic Director of York Theatre Royal for the past six years. In that time he has directed many productions including: *Brassed Off, Caitlin, Habeas Corpus; Up 'n' Under; Frankenstein; Noises Off; Little Shop of Horrors; Othello; Closer; The Turn of the Screw; Bedevilled; A Funny Thing Happened on the Way to the Forum; Behind the Scenes at the Museum; Bouncers; Kafka's Dick; Man of the Moment; Having a Ball; Romeo and Juliet; Getting On; The Three Musketeers; Les Liaisons Dangereuses; All My Sons; Piaf; Dead Funny; Educating Rita; Frankie and Johnnie at the Claire De Lune; Neville's Island; Multiplex; Abandonment; Private Lives.*

Before York, Damian worked for various regional theatres as a freelance director and was Associate Director for Hull Truck. He trained at the Royal Scottish Academy of Music and Drama between 1982 and 1986.

Christopher Madin Composer, arranger and sound design

Christopher's composition work for York Theatre Royal includes: *Brassed Off*, *The Pocket Dream*, *Caitlin*, *Private Lives*, *Abandonment*, *All My Sons*, *A Midsummer Night's Dream*, *Othello*, *The Blue Room*, *The Three Musketeers*, *Behind the Scenes at the Museum*, *The Chrysalids*, *Habeas Corpus*, *Up 'n' Under*, *The Glass Menagerie*, *Frankenstein*, *The Snow Queen*, *Having a Ball*, *Bouncers*, *Disco Pigs* and *Romeo and Juliet*. Credits for other theatres include: *The Lifeblood*, Edinburgh Festival; *Romeo and Juliet* and *The Snow Queen*, Crucible Theatre, Sheffield; *Passion Killers, Up 'n' Under 2*, *Bouncers* and *Laurel and Hardy*, Hull Truck Theatre; and *Beauty and The Beast*, Chester Gateway.

Christopher also composes music for Compass Theatre Company, including the current tour of *The Rivals*. His work for television and radio includes, *Two Lives, One Body* for ITV and, *Behind the Scenes at the Museum*, and the classic serialisation of *The Midwich Cuckoos* (nominated for the Sony International Radio Drama Award) for Radio Four.

Elizabeth Mansfield Lili Brik

Elizabeth trained at Elmhurst Ballet School; Guildhall School of Music and Drama; City of Leeds College of Music.

Theatre credits include: Red Ladder Theatre; *Piaf*, York Theatre Royal; *The Mother*, BAC/National tour; *Women of Troy*, Royal National Theatre; *True Brit*, Birmingham Repertory; *Flora The Red Menace*, *Nutmeg & Ginger*, Orange Tree, Richmond; *Hymn to Love*, Drill Hall, London/Mercury, Colchester/Traverse, Edinburgh; *China Song*, Theatre Royal Plymouth; *The Threepenny Opera*, Contact, Manchester; *Grave Plots*, Nottingham Playhouse; *Marie*, Fortune Theatre, London/National & USA tour (Best Actress in a Musical nomination Olivier Awards/London Theatre Critic's Awards 1996); *Portraits in Song*, National & USA tour; *Ludwig's Ghosts* (with the Peabody Trio), London/Washington DC/New York.

Elizabeth has recorded many plays for BBC Radio. Her television credits include *Casualty*; *Bluebell*; *Fringe Benefits*; *The Bill*; *1914 All Out*; *Coronation Street*.

Robert Pickavance Osip Brik

Robert read History at York and Oxford Universities.

His theatre credits include: *Huddersfield* and *Coming Around Again*, West Yorkshire Playhouse; *Bedtime Stories*, *Neville's Island*, *Road*, *Educating Rita* and *Romeo and Juliet*, York Theatre Royal; *Dracula*, *What the Butler Saw* and *Who's Afraid of Virginia Woolf*, Duke's Theatre, Lancaster; *Taming of the Shrew* and *Mrs Warren's Profession*, Royal Exchange, Manchester; *Anna Karenina*, *Neville's Island*, *A Christmas Carol* and *The Norman Conquests*, Octagon Theatre, Bolton; *Foe*, Complicité; *Cyrano de Bergerac* and *Carmen*, Communicado.

Robert's theatre credits as a director include: *Woman In Mind*, Octagon Theatre, Bolton; *Look Back In Anger* and *Not About Heroes*, Duke's Theatre, Lancaster; and *Antigone*, Communicado.

His television credits include: *Foyle's War*; *Kavanagh QC*; *Gas Attack*; *Midsomer Murders*; and *City Central.*

John Sackville Vladimir Mayakovsky

Trained at Webber Douglas after being awarded the McEuen Acting Prize for the title rôle in *Hamlet* at the Scottish Student Drama Festival.

Theatre includes: the British Premières of *Reader*, by Ariel Dorfman, Oval Theatre, London and *Party*, Arts Theatre, London; *Othello* and *Volpone*, RSC; *Lone Flyer* and *Witch* (Peter Brook Empty Space Award), Watermill Theatre, tour and Warehouse Theatre, Croydon; *The Duchess of Malfi*, Byre Theatre, St. Andrews; *Hamlet*, Oxford Stage Company; *Forty Years On*, *Spider's Web* and the World Première of *Funny Money*, Palace Theatre, Westcliff; *Cause Célèbre*, *Charley's Aunt*, *Building Blocks*, *A Chorus of Disapproval* and the World Première of *First Class Passengers*, Pitlochry Festival Theatre; *Emma*, Wimbledon Theatre and tour; *Cyrano de Bergerac* and *Our Country's Good*, Nuffield Theatre, Southampton.

TV credits include: *The Royal*, *Heartbeat*, *The Bill* and *Midsomer Murders.* Film credits include: *Something Borrowed*, *My Kind of Girl* and *The Mosquito, The Flea, The Fly*.

Gilly Tompkins Annushka

Gilly trained at Bretton Hall College.

Her theatre credits include: *Fly Me To The Moon*, Stephen Joseph Theatre, Scarborough; *Noises Off*, York Theatre Royal *Get Shortie*, *Live Bed Show* and *House and Garden*, Northampton Theatre; *Sexing Alan Titchmarsh*, Pleasance, Edinburgh Festival; *Thick As A Brick*, Hull Truck & Greenwich Theatre; *Talking Heads*, Northcott Theatre, Exeter; *Absent Friends*, Greenwich Theatre; *Absurd Person Singular* and *Office Party*, Palace Theatre, Watford; *Time of My Life*, Derby Playhouse; *Gym & Tonic*, *Passion Killers*, *Blood Sweat & Tears*, Hull Truck & Derby Playhouse; *Enjoy*, Nottingham Playhouse; *On The Piste*, Garrick Theatre; and *Teechers*, Arts Theatre.

Gilly's television credits include: *The Queen's Nose*; *Eastenders*; *Casualty*; *Victoria Wood Show*; *Birds of a Feather* and *Barbara.*

Film credits include: *Act of Will*; *The Human Bomb*; and *Girl's Night*.

Steve Trafford Writer

Steve read English at Sussex University.

A founder member of Red Ladder Theatre, Steve wrote and co-wrote their work, including: *Nerves of Steel* (dir: Chris Rawlence), *Taking Our Time* (dir: Michael Attenborough), *Ladders to the Moon* (dir: Annie Castledine). Further theatre work includes *Marie- The Story of Marie Lloyd*, also adapted for BBC Radio 4, and *Hymn To Love – Homage to Piaf*, including his new translations of Piaf's greatest songs, adapted for BBC Radio 3. Steve translated Brecht's *The Mother*, for a major national tour, with songs set to Hanns Eisler's original score.

He scripted the Channel 4 feature film *T Dan. Smith* for Amber Films, and has written many popular TV series including: *The Bill*, *The Knock*, *Midsomer Murders*, and the BBC series *Between the Lines*, winning a Writer's Guild Award.

A CLOUD IN TROUSERS

Following performances at The Studio, York Theatre Royal, 1–23 October 2004, the production tours to:

New Vic Theatre, Newcastle under Lyme	28 October
Merlin Theatre, Frome	30 October
The Lighthouse, Poole	1–2 November
The Southwark Playhouse, London	4–20 November
Theatre by the Lake, Keswick	22–23 November
Clwyd Theatr Cymru, Mold	25–26 November
Marsden Theatre, Leyland	27 November
Angles Theatre, Wisbech	1 December
Leighton Buzzard Theatre	2 December
Burton Taylor Studio, Oxford Playhouse	6–7 December
Ustinov Studio, Theatre Royal Bath	9–11 December

Ensemble

Ensemble was formed in 2000 by Elizabeth Mansfield and Steve Trafford to create and tour new theatre work, exploring the relationship between music and text, within a multi-cultural perspective.

They began their collaboration working in the Red Ladder Theatre Company, which toured original music theatre pieces to non-theatrical venues. They went on to create *Marie –The Story of Marie Lloyd*, which began at the Edinburgh Festival and then toured the UK, the USA and Norway. *Marie* was also produced at the Fortune Theatre in London, where Elizabeth was nominated for an Olivier Award. They created Hymn to Love – Homage to Piaf, with Annie Castledine, and in 2000 produced a national tour of *The Mother* by Bertolt Brecht, in a new translation by Steve Trafford.

Since the formation of Ensemble, the company has produced five new pieces of theatre work: *Portraits in Song*, *The Uninvited*, *Ludwig's Ghosts*, *The Greatest Drummer in the World*, *A Cloud in Trousers*. Currently in development are *The Woman in Red* (working title) with The Saam Studio, and *Circles of Chalk*, a new play by Steve Trafford.

Our artistic collaborators include: Richard Aylwin, Simon Banham, Nick Beadle, Russell Churney, Judith Cloke, Damian Cruden, Soussan Farrokhnia, Rachana Jadhav, Christopher Madin, Anna Mudeka, Naoko Nagai, The Peabody Trio (Natasha Brofsky, Seth Knopp, Violaine Melançon), Robert Pickavance, John Sackville, Mustafa Shafafi, Javhad Shams, Gilly Tompkins, Leon Rosselson and Tim Sutton.

September 2004.

For further information visit Ensemble's website at:
www.ensemble-online.com

Ensemble Limited
Registered Office: 105 Thames Side, Staines, Middlesex TW18 2HG

York Theatre Royal
The Studio

York Theatre Royal is one of the country's leading repertory companies. Over the last three years we have established links with leading theatre companies. both as venue partner, and as collaborator through co-productions. Our relationship with Ensemble and other touring companies allows us to produce new work in our Studio space, and to assist in the development of quality writing. We hope therefore that the benefits brought to our own community in York, in this way, will also be shared across the country. We are grateful to Arts Council England for their contribution to this project, enabling this new piece to tour nationally. We are currently engaged with several other companies, and hope to develop this model of good practice still further.

Damian Cruden Artistic Director

York Theatre Royal Staff

Chief Executive **Ludo Keston**
Artistic Director **Damian Cruden**

Administration

General Manager **Vicky Biles**
PA to the directors **Kelly Smith**
Head of Accounts **John Renel**
Payroll Officer **Jane Travis**
Cashier **Jackie Raper**
Accounts Assistant **Claire Flanagan**
IT Support Officer **Matt Savage**
Receptionist **Carol Morrill**

Education

Director of Education **Jill Adamson**
Youth Theatre Director **Sarah Brigham**
Education Associates **Stephen Burke***, **Lee Threadgold**
Education Administrator **Lucy Crux-Walsh**
Catalyst Associate† **Sian Williams**
Education placement **Lauran Ransom**

Marketing

Head of Marketing and Business Development **Vicky Petrie**
Marketing Officer **Anna Mitchelson**
Public Relations Officer **Duncan Clarke**
Marketing Assistant **Lizzie Glazier**
Box Office Supervisor **Rachel Naylor**
Box Office Assistants **Anna Boaden¶, Judy Dickinson¶, Ann Forshaw,
Pam Lydiate¶, Isy Mead¶, Catherine Taylor**

Production

Production Manager **Matt Noddings**
Technical Manager **Jamie Molyneaux**
Stage Manager **Anna Belderbos**
Deputy Stage Managers **Amy Bending, Emma Clare**
Assistant Stage Manager **Tony Topping**
Chief Electrician **Judith Cloke**
Assistant Electricians **Christopher Randall, David Simpson**
Stage Technicians **Terry Bounds, Andy Furey**
Stage Door Keepers **Brian Morrison, Simon Overton**
Propmaker **Michael Roberts**
Head of Wardrobe **Juliette Berry**
Deputy Head of Wardrobe **Audrey George**
Cutter **Paula Grosvenor**
Wardrobe Assistants **Shay Daly, Helen Russell**
Wardrobe Assistant and Maintenance **Catherine Chapman**
Costume Hire Supervisor ¶ **Pauline Rourke**

Front of House

Front of House Manager **Kaeli Moorhouse**
Duty Managers ¶ **Maria Bewers, Madeleine Frost, Rachel Naylor**
Maintenance Technician **Richard Cregan**
Ushers ¶ **Kareen Andrews, Maria Bewers, Jenna Eames, Jeanette
Elwell, Sam Freeman, Jean McDonald, Danielle Nassau, Sylvia
Nicholls, Adam Nicolle, Stephanie Nicolle, Pat Norton, Lucy
Popplewell, Rita Ridgeon, Jilly Stephenson, Sarah Warren.**
Cleaning Supervisor ¶ **Carole Lock**
Cleaners ¶ **Carol Collingwood, Ivan Goa, Bo Han, Deanne Lincoln,
Kathleen Stubbs, Desmond Wu, Catherine Xie.**

Catering

Catering Manager **Chris Scott**
Bar Supervisor **Michaela Scott**
Cafe Bar Assistants¶
Lisa Blankley, Glen Brett, Karen Burborough, Claire Coulson, Danielle Dawson, Jasmine Field, Andy Furby, Georgina Hope, Vicky Knipe, Jonathan Spratley, Nicola Tate, Sarah Warren, Sarah Welles, Karen Winlow

Audio Describers

Helen Anderson, Maureen Dow, Chris Gallagher, Jenny Major, Peter Taylor, Jacqui Taylor, Susan Towle.

Members of the Board

Chair of the Board: Professor Dianne Willcocks

Members of the Board
David Dickson, (Vice-Chair), David Brooks, Gillian Cruddas, Tricia Ellison, Cllr David Evans, Cllr Madeleine Kirk , Kevin Lavery, , Dennis MacDonald, Cllr. Quentin Macdonald, Cllr Carol Runciman, Cllr. David Wilde, Tina Wright

Company Secretary
Cllr Janet Looker

¶ Denotes part-time position
* York Theatre Royal gratefully acknowledges the support of the City of York Council in the funding of this position.
† York Theatre Royal gratefully acknowledges the support of the York Children's Fund in the funding of this position.

Steve Trafford

A CLOUD IN TROUSERS

OBERON BOOKS
LONDON

This adaptation first published in 2004 by Oberon Books Ltd
521 Caledonian Road, London N7 9RH
Tel: 020 7607 3637 / Fax: 020 7607 3629
e-mail: oberon.books@btinternet.com
www.oberonbooks.com

A catalogue record for this book is available from the British
Library.

ISBN: 1 84002 506 9

Cover graphic concept: Simon Williams Design
                      www.simonwilliams.co.uk

Printed in Great Britain by Antony Rowe Ltd, Chippenham.

CHARACTERS

VLADIMIR MAYAKOVSKY

LILI BRIK

OSIP BRIK

ANNUSHKA

Author's note

Permission to use the translations of Mayakovsky's poetry contained in this production has been kindly granted by Ann and Sam Charters, whose book *I Love* (ISBN: 0 233 97070 3) is an excellent account of the relationship between Lili Brik and Mayakovsky. Also, permissions have been granted by the Princeton University Press to use extracts from *Mayakovsky* by Edward J Brown (ISBN: 0 691 06255 2), a fascinating analysis of Mayakovsky's verse.

Special thanks to: John Banks, Andrina Carroll, Suzy Cooper, Annie Castledine, Damian Cruden, Heather Davies, Elissa Guralnick, Roger McCann, Leonie Mellinger, Robert Pickavance, Nigel Richards, Timothy Sutton, Tim Welton.

ACT ONE

Scene One

MAYAKOVSKY appears, dressed in an overcoat (as in the final scene.).
He takes out a gun and spins the chamber.
He holds the gun to his head.

MAYAKOVSKY: Quiet! You will be quiet. Quiet like flowers.

> *Music.*
> *TITLE: '1915'*
> *TITLE: 'A man from the future'*
> *MAYAKOVSKY laughs. He pockets the gun and produces a flower and holds it toward members of the audience.*

Look… Feel… Smell… You like the pansy's perfume?

MAYAKOVSKY eats the flower.

I have swallowed beauty. My flowers are an angry bouquet of prostitutes. Punctuation does not exist in the continuous dynamism of thought like the dance of the object in film my words are forward motions fevered steps somersaulting and slapping the face of taste with the blow of a fist. (*Pause.*) He's smirking. (*Shrugs.*) The horse who first saw a camel laughed himself hoarse!

MAYAKOVSKY takes off his overcoat and throws it away, revealing a colourful futurist waistcoat.

It's hot. I'm earning my crust here. All workers have the right to improve their working conditions. Tonight, there will be an interval for me to rest and for you to express your delight to each other.

Music.

october the 8th
1915
the date
when time watched the ritual scene
of my initiation as a soldier
you hear
everyone
unneeded even
must live
you hear me
must
no one
into the graves of trenches
while living
murderers
must be thrust
if you want now shoot me
to a pole tie me tighter
I won't even change in my face
if you like
for the target to burn brighter
to my forehead I'll stick an ace

Spit o wind, an armful of leaves! I am a hooligan like
you!!

you wallowing in orgy after orgy
owning a bathroom and a warm loo
how does it feel reading about the awards of St George
from the papers in your morning rooms
do you know insensitive nonentities
thinking only of filling your gobs
that this moment the legs of Petrov the lieutenant
were ripped off by a bomb
to give my life for the likes of you
lips drooling with lust
I'd rather serve pineapple booze
to the whores in Moscow bars.
who am I?

I'm a man of no class
no nation
no tribe
I've seen the thirtieth
and the fortieth centuries
I am simply a man
   from the future

Exit MAYAKOVSKY.
Music continues.

Scene Two

TITLE: 'a cloud in trousers'
Music.
An easel, a telephone. LILI dancing. She moves to the easel and begins to paint.
Enter OSIP BRIK with a newspaper...

OSIP: The power in words, Lili!

LILI: What?

   The music ends.

OSIP: He put three single syllable words on the lips of millions and they have written a revolution: 'Bread, Peace and Land!' Lenin is brilliant.

   Enter ANNUSHKA with a bentwood chair.

LILI: Will it be more than words, this time?

OSIP: The front's already collapsed into the rear. The army's voting with its feet. There'll be civil war with the Cossacks.

ANNUSHKA: Basil the Blessed preserve us! Another war!? If 'revolution' means the Cossacks coming here, you can keep it. That lot'll set fire to the city just to see better what they're doing.

LILI: No Nushka… The revolution will mean freedom. For everyone. No serfs, slaves, or servants…

ANNUSHKA: That's me out of a job, then!

ANNUSHKA starts sawing the chair.

ANNUSHKA: I was talking to Maria Alexevna, the nurse in number twenty three, this morning… She was telling me: A train from the front reached the railway station. In one car there were forty lads. Three legs between them. Amputation's a tricky business. Before you cut through the bone, you have to cut the muscles, pull back the flesh with tongs, and then saw the leg clean off, without splinters. Otherwise the bone grows again and pierces the stump…

LILI: Annushka!

ANNUSHKA: If you don't like to hear this, don't talk to me about revolution.

OSIP: (*Realisation.*) Is that my chair?!!

ANNUSHKA: No… It's soup. You want to sit or eat? This is the last wood.

OSIP sighs.

ANNUSHKA: The lads said the British, Turks and French are still fighting the Germans. But not us…we're fighting each other. The Georgians falling out with the Russians, the Ukranians breaking the Latvians' heads, and the Jews are hanging about sulking, waiting to be beaten up.

OSIP: Well… No point being frozen when we're surrounded by dead wood. Here… *The Cherry Orchard.* Chop it up… (*Slings a book to the stove.*) While you're at it… Burn Chekhov's bloody whining sisters… *War and Peace…* You can't read a book like that without a sofa to lounge on… (*Throws it.*)

ANNUSHKA: This'll burn better than a bone dry log. The fat ones are best.

OSIP: Annushka!! You should be made Professor of Literary Criticism. Burn the lot! From now on *we* will be our own ancestors.

ANNUSHKA: I can't fathom him sometimes, Lilichka. He reads everything, but talks about books like a cook wringing a chicken's neck.

LILI laughs.

OSIP: Here… Tolstoy, Pushkin… They'll keep us warm. The age will no longer be a wild animal, with a broken backbone, looking round at its own footprints.

ANNUSHKA: True enough…

OSIP: From now on… (*For LILI's benefit.*) Art will serve life…

Exit OSIP.
Music.
LILI resumes dancing.
A knocking.
Enter MAYAKOVSKY wearing a top coat, with a tie pinned to the shoulder. He carries a cane.

MAYAKOVSKY: I'm looking for Elsa.

ANNUSHKA: (*Suspicious.*) Who are you?

MAYAKOVSKY: My card…

MAYAKOVSKY produces a large calling card from inside his topcoat and shows it to ANNUSHKA. It reads: 'Vladimir Mayakovsky. Celebrated poet and artist'. ANNUSHKA cannot read.

ANNUSHKA: What's that?

MAYAKOVSKY: 'Vladimir Mayakovsky, celebrated poet and artist.'

ANNUSHKA: Never heard of you!

MAYAKOVSKY: Fame grows like a dead man's beard, after death. While I'm alive, I shave.

ANNUSHKA: Bugger off…

MAYAKOVSKY: I'll leave my card and count on you to deliver it.

ANNUSHKA: You'll be counting the stairs with your arse if you don't go now!

MAYAKOVSKY pushes past ANNUSHKA.

MAYAKOVSKY: (*To LILI.*) Good afternoon. (*Bows.*)

ANNUSHKA: Sorry Madame Lili. He barged in.

The music stops.

MAYAKOVSKY: Vladimir Mayakovsky…

ANNUSHKA: Says he's famous…

LILI and MAYAKOVSKY stare at each other

ANNUSHKA: (*Flat disdain.*) I'll make the tea then.

MAYAKOVSKY: Some honey for me…

ANNUSHKA looks askance and goes.

LILI: My sister's not here. She has no wish to see you again.

MAYAKOVSKY: Elsa spoke of me…?

LILI: Oh yes…

MAYAKOVSKY: What words did she use?

LILI: She said that within five minutes of meeting her, you took her in your arms and told her how wonderful you are.

MAYAKOVSKY: I believe it was ten minutes, but time *was* standing still. The stale bread of yesterday's caress still sticks to my lips. She kissed me. Here.

MAYAKOVSKY lifts the painting LILI has been working on. It is of a child.

Your daughter?

LILI: No. This is Natasha Brodsky. A child from the bicycle factory…

MAYAKOVSKY: Is it a good 'likeness'?

LILI: I think so…

MAYAKOVSKY: The purpose of art is to make the familiar, unfamiliar.

LILI: What do *you* paint?

MAYAKOVSKY: At the School of Art everybody was painting angels, I wanted to paint flies. But after electricity came, I lost all interest in nature. Not up to date enough.

LILI: Why do you wear your tie on your shoulder?

MAYAKOVSKY: Is there a more sensible place to wear a tie?

LILI: Round your neck perhaps?

MAYAKOVSKY: Did you hear about the man who was hanged for stealing a horse? On the gallows, as they slipped the rope around his neck, his last words, shouted to the crowd, were: 'Drink Van Heutens Cocoa!' The manufacturers had agreed to pay his family a fat fee. There were three thousand people watching! The Press published! It is always important to die *usefully*.

OSIP enters with an armful of books.

LILI: Olya, this is Mr Vladimir Mayakovsky. 'Celebrated artist and poet'.

MAYAKOVSKY: Streets are my brushes, squares are my palettes. I paint the summer lightning of the new coming beauty with words.

OSIP: Who sent you?

MAYAKOVSKY: The Future.

LILI: He's looking for Elsa. Another jilted lover.

MAYAKOVSKY: I will read for you. (*Produces a book of poems made of wrapping paper.*)

Music.

OSIP: Not now. I have business…

MAYAKOVSKY: Please… More terrible than a bullet in the head is that 'from-you-to-here' silence.

The music underscores.

Gentle ones
You yearn your love on a violin
The crude beat their love on a drum
But no one can like me turn outside in
And nothing but human lips become.
If you like
I'll be furious flesh resentful
Or changing to tones that the sunset arouses
I'll be extraordinarily gentle
Not a man – but a cloud in trousers.

The music stops.

OSIP: Where did you learn to write like that?

LILI takes MAYAKOVSKY's notebook.

MAYAKOVSKY: In prison. I dug a tunnel to release the women from Taganka jail. They nabbed me. I plunged into words in solitary cell 103. Byron, Shakespeare, *Anna Karenina*. But they came in the night and told me to pack my things. Never did find out how that Karenina business ended.

OSIP: You're a Lyricist…?

MAYAKOVSKY: They're crippled with rhymatism. Now is not the time for poets to lie in their bedrooms, wooing the daisies on the wall.

LILI: Osip… Listen…

Music.
LILI reads from notebook.

Today you must
With a knuckle duster
Beat this world's thick skull…

MAYAKOVSKY takes over reciting his poem by heart.
LILI hands the book to OSIP, who follows the text, as:

MAYAKOVSKY:
Pub crawlers pull your hands from your pants
Grab bombs, cobblestones, scythes or instead
Those of you who haven't got arms or hands
Batter at the walls with your heads
Skewer this life with gutting knives
You who were vulgarised and trample
This world
Bloated with Rothchild's pudding wives
Over-fed and pampered
To arms on lamp posts hoist them higher
Shop keepers and bloody parasites
New flags to flutter in the fever of fire
Your feast day roar our proper rites.

The music stops.

OSIP: Have you shown your work to anyone else?

MAYAKOVSKY: To Gorky. He wept.

LILI: Gorky weeps reading his electricity bill!

OSIP: Are you published?

MAYAKOVSKY: Only on wrapping paper. And alive, in the Stray Dog café, every night. Sawdust on the floor and me on the stage.

OSIP: It's possible… I could get you published…

MAYAKOVSKY: You're a printer?

LILI: Osip is a critic…

MAYAKOVSKY: Oh… I met a critic once. At one of my plays. He was mad. Participating in a sublime experience and at the same time making notes. The doctors diagnosed schizophrenia. The man was a chicken who thought he could teach ducks to swim.

OSIP: I know as much about swimming as a man with no arms…but I do think there's a science in every art, worth discerning.

MAYAKOVSKY: Don't understand science. I never grasped the theory of gravity. Not till the ceiling fell on my head.

OSIP: (*Sparring.*) I'm for tearing down ceilings.

MAYAKOVSKY: Good. They prevent you from seeing the stars. (*Beat.*) Frankly, I despise Critics! Bathing attendants at literary spas. Pouring warm baths for the bourgeois to soak in.

OSIP: I tend to the Archimedes school of criticism. We should be elephants who roar and stick our feet in warm tubs, so when they're pulled out, there's no water left for the old and tired to wallow in.

MAYAKOVSKY: Ha! What art do you like?

OSIP: I prefer cubism and don't give a damn-ism to pictures of bowls of fruit. I love words that are bread not sticky cakes. Art that transforms life down to the last buttons on your clothes. And you?

MAYAKOVSKY: When I open 'great' books I fall asleep. I go to a play and want to scream 'the Emperors have no clothes'. The theatres are clogged with second rate directors milking emaciated dogs… They're afraid of the new.

LILI: You write plays, too?

MAYAKOVSKY: Not lately. They have told the living not to bother writing plays. They have dead men who do that.

OSIP: The boy who shouted 'the Emperor has no clothes' was lucky. He said it at the right time, in the right place. Fairy tales are one thing, life is another.

MAYAKOVSKY: Which means?

OSIP: My friend, there is no point in writing if you are not read. To be published, you must join the Party now.

MAYAKOVSKY: I am answerable only to the Future.

OSIP: Soon, you'll be answerable to the District Committee. We all will. I have a meeting to attend.

He kisses LILI and gives her back the notebook, as:

OSIP: I'll see you tonight… (*To MAYAKOVSKY.*) Leave your work with us… (*The 'Book'.*) We must talk further.

Exit OSIP.

MAYAKOVSKY: So… He's a Bolshevik?

LILI: Osip…is in the party.

MAYAKOVSKY: I intend to publish myself… I've put in a request to the Dumas for two hundred reams.

LILI: Paper is scarce. Such requests are spiked at the post office.

MAYAKOVSKY: Mine won't be. You see, I included a demand that the wages of all telegraph operators be doubled. They'll send it through.

LILI reading the notebook.

LILI: This is wonderful love poetry…

MAYAKOVSKY: Love poetry is smouldering hearts and posies of roses. When something smoulders, I call the fire department. I look for 'roses' in horticultural books.

LILI: There's no shame in writing about love… You do it magnificently…

MAYAKOVSKY: Do I?

LILI: (*Reads.*)
Maria…again
Downcast and alone

Music.

I'll take my heart
Wrapped in tears of pain
And carry it
Like a dog
Who drags
To his kennel home
A paw run over by a train
Almighty! A pair of hands you invented
Arranged for everyone
A head like this
Why didn't you see to it
That without being in pain tormented
We could
Kiss and kiss and kiss…

MAYAKOVSKY speaks the last 'kiss and kiss' with LILI.

The music stops.

Who was she? Maria?

MAYAKOVSKY: A woman. I waited for her. Rain trickled down the window and I melted the pane with my brow. I walked all night.

LILI: And now?

MAYAKOVSKY: Gone. Married a dealer in soft fruit. 'A ring… Look… I'm getting married…' 'OK, get married. Fine! I can take it. You see how calm I am. Calm as a dead man's pulse.' I wasn't suitable for her…

LILI: You probably frightened her to death.

MAYAKOVSKY: Do I frighten you?

LILI: No…

MAYAKOVSKY: Maria possessed me. She drove me to the brink like the moon draws a sleep-walker to the roof.

Pause.

MAYAKOVSKY: Osip… He is your husband?

LILI: Yes.

MAYAKOVSKY: Are you Jews?

LILI: Yes… But it's alright, we eat bacon.

MAYAKOVSKY: Good. Nobody should obey the rules anymore… Where did you find him?

LILI: At a study group on Marxism.

MAYAKOVSKY: And fell passionately in love…

LILI: Not exactly. He took me to see a film. Brought a friend. They sat either side of me. Osip smuggled his hand into the end of the fur muff that lay on my lap. His friend slipped his hand in the other end. All

29

through the film they each dabbled each other's fingers, and stroked, and squeezed…each other's hands. Both looked at me, but I watched the film, my hands in the pocket of my gown…

MAYAKOVSKY: Could you love me, Lili?

Music.

LILI: Don't be absurd!

MAYAKOVSKY: You don't want to answer… but you like the question?

Enter ANNUSHKA with tea.

Let's dance. A tea dance! Our feet will be feathers. A gavotte in praise of buoyancy. Annushka, dance with us!

ANNUSHKA: I've got feet like loaf tins.

ANNUSHKA goes.

MAYAKOVSKY: Come Lili…

MAYAKOVSKY and LILI together, dancing. They dance off.
The music segues into:

Scene Three

TITLE: 'the thunder of wheels and the whisper of shoes'
The phone ringing.
ANNUSHKA picks up the phone.

ANNUSHKA: 67-10… Who's calling?

OSIP hurries in.

ANNUSHKA: It's for you…

OSIP: Who is it?

ANNUSHKA: Them, I think.

OSIP takes the phone. Exit ANNUSHKA.

OSIP: (*On phone.*) Brik… Yes, Comrade… It is arranged…
… Of course… I'm working on it with him now…
Tomorrow… (*Phone down.*)

The music stops.
*MAYAKOVSKY enters carrying a marked up text of his
poem 'Clouds'.*

MAYAKOVSKY: What are these dots!? These little hooks
stuck in my verse? You have destroyed it!

OSIP: I have edited it… The printers are waiting…

MAYAKOVSKY: (*Angry.*) Have you ever written
anything!?

OSIP: Yes…

MAYAKOVSKY: Then mess about with that! You come
and put your grubby marks on words I've crafted,
sweated blood over!

OSIP: It was obscure.

MAYAKOVSKY: The undisturbed rhythm of words is their
meaning: the thunder of wheels the whisper of shoes.
Each thing invades the other, in art as in life!

OSIP: Syntax and punctuation are the architecture of
meaning.

MAYAKOVSKY: I don't write like that!

OSIP: Then how do you write?

MAYAKOVSKY: To the echo of my soul. For me, writing
is making love with my entire being.

OSIP: You write with ink, not blood. A scientific
understanding must underpin everything. (*Pause.*) Have
you read Pavlov, Volodya?

MAYAKOVSKY: What?

31

OSIP: The dog man.

MAYAKOVSKY: I love dogs. He drives them mad I hear.

OSIP: For a purpose. Pavlov argues that reality is understood by stimuli in the brain, transmitted by the visual and aural cells to the cortex, by the organs of perception.

MAYAKOVSKY: Oh… You think writing's a cerebral business?

OSIP: Like dog's brains, *we* have the same primary signal system. But there is a secondary system in us, and that is the 'word'. A signal of the primary signal, that takes us beyond automatic, animal responses: hunger, terror, desire …

MAYAKOVSKY: I've read my poetry to dogs. They howl.

OSIP: I am speaking scientifically. *Words* bring perception to the highest possible intensity. Beyond reflex feelings to perception that can change reality. Change minds. Words are revolution.

MAYAKOVSKY: When the temperature falls below 32 degrees, the ink in my inkwell freezes. That's also scientific.

OSIP: You write with passion. But too much of your tortured soul. It simply prompts feelings. Is that why you write? So that men will reach for their handkerchiefs and leave their brains behind?

MAYAKOVSKY: What do you want of me?

OSIP: To write words that make men think. Make men act…

MAYAKOVSKY: Rabble rousing stuff!? Clunking agitprop? I can't write poetry to order. There are no rules about counting stars while riding a bicycle.

OSIP: Are you a circus clown!?

MAYAKOVSKY: I am an artist.

OSIP: Yes. But this (*'Clouds'.*) is written for people like us. We're already bloated with words. You say you're against salon culture and easel painting. All that deadly stuff?

MAYAKOVSKY: I abhor every kind of deathliness, adore every kind of new life, and love. There's not one single grey hair in my soul.

OSIP: Then, be a writer for the revolution. Homer wrote about the wars of Troy. Why not write about the guns of October? Write rhythms that echo the roar of the streets, the din of intense production. The Revolution needs Constructive Art, slogans, in factories, in newspapers…

MAYAKOVSKY: A newspaper's fine for the morning, what about the evening?

OSIP: In the evening, evening newspapers. This is magnificent! It must be published. But too much of it is beyond the masses' understanding.

MAYAKOVSKY: So what? The universe waited millions of years for Kepler to come and understand it. I can wait a few decades to be appreciated…

OSIP: No! The battle is raging now. If we don't fight for a future art, a revolutionary art, it will die in the Gulags. I have Pasternak, Schlovsky, Rodchenko…we are forming a Left Front for Art. You must join us.

MAYAKOVSKY: And be herded with the herd!

OSIP: We're swept by a river, Volodya, and all wisdom resides in riding the current, not being washed aside. We need raw art, new words. Not the stream of fancy, the river of fact, brimming with the urgent questions of change.

Music.

MAYAKOVSKY:
> How can I explain to you
> My state of mind?
> If I were not a poet
> I would be a stargazer.
> To love means this: to run
> Into the depths of a yard
> And, till the rook-black night,
> Chop wood with a shining axe
> Giving full play to one's strength.
> To love is to break away from bedsheets
> Torn by insomnia jealous of the moon
> Love for me is no paradise of arbors
> To me, love tells us, humming
> That the stalled motor of the heart
> Has started to work again.
> To lift up and lead and entice
> Those who have grown weak in the eye
> To saw from the shoulders hostile heads
> With the tail of a glittering sword.
> Love human and simple
> Hurricane, fire, water
> Surging forward, rumbling.
> Who can control this?
> Can you? Try it…

Music segues into:

Scene Four

TITLE: 'when the rivers of the world splash honey'

LILI: (*Sings.*)
> Love for me is no paradise of arbors
> To me, love tells us, humming
> That the stalled motor of the heart
> Has started to work again.

The music ends.
OSIP is alone marking up a text.
LILI carries a basket of washed nappies.
LILI begins to put up a wash line.

OSIP: Lili… I want you to talk to Mayakovsky. Persuade him to join the Left Front… He refuses.

LILI: He's not the sort to join anything: whatever it is he'll be against it, on principle.

OSIP: We need him. The Party's idea of popular culture is balalaika musicals at the national theatre and publishing the memoirs of plumbers. Nothing to frighten the sheep, or the comrades of the Central Committee…

LILI: He's more alive than all of them put together.

OSIP: And we must keep him alive…

LILI: What do you mean?

OSIP: He's arrogant, Lili, and reckless. His head's that swollen with his own words he can hardly get his cap on.

LILI: He's a wild bird. You won't cage him.

OSIP: I want him to fly. His poetry is more muscular, and more powerful than…Pushkin's. He will make enemies in dangerous places. You have an 'affection' for him, don't you?

LILI: Yes…

OSIP: And he for you. Persuade him to join the Left Front for Art. None of us can live only for ourselves, now, Lili. Persuade him… In whatever way you can…

LILI looks at OSIP.
Enter ANNUSHKA with a straw bag. Exit OSIP.

ANNUSHKA: The market was heaving. Flies buzzing over crumbs. No bread. And those damn peasants, cunning Christ kissers, are sat there cross legged, hoarding their vegetables behind beards the size of shields.

LILI: You got nothing?

ANNUSHKA: (*Empties bag.*) One cabbage…which has been a maternity home for maggots. Half a thumb of stale sausage. And four potatoes, with more wires than a telephone exchange. And an apple.

LILI: Did you get me gloves?

ANNUSHKA shakes head.

None to be had anywhere?

ANNUSHKA: No… No clothes…and one apple between all of us. We're in paradise alright!

The phone rings.
Music.
ANNUSHKA and LILI look at it and wait. The ringing stops in mid-ring.
The music stops.
ANNUSHKA gathers up the vegetables. LILI hangs up nappies.

Madame Lili… Would you talk to Master Osip about putting in a word? About my son, Nikolai…

LILI: Is he in trouble?

ANNUSHKA: Not of his own making. His regiment's run out of ammunition. He says all they're getting sent is bad cocoa and worse blankets. I want him transferred back to Moscow, before he gets put to bed with a shovel.

LILI: I doubt Osip can do anything for him…

ANNUSHKA: I was thinking maybe the Cheka could help?

LILI: What makes you think Osip has any influence with them?

ANNUSHKA: Well…all these calls he gets…they're from the Lubianka, aren't they?

LILI: Have you been listening in?!

ANNUSHKA: No… They leave messages… For Master Osip to call.

LILI: Osip has been doing some legal drafting work for the Office of the Political Police, that's all… He has no influence there.

ANNUSHKA: I just thought, seeing as how we got the electricity fixed up on the Reserve cable…somebody must love us?

LILI: I will speak to Osip…about your son, but never, ever, repeat anything you see, or overhear, in this apartment to anyone, Annushka. Phone calls, visitors, anything. Is that clear?

ANNUSHKA: Yes, Madame Lili…

LILI: Keep a bridle on that tongue of yours.

ANNUSHKA exits.

MAYAKOVKY: (*Entering.*) What's she been saying?

LILI: Oh just some loose gossip she picked up at the market.

MAYAKOVSKY: Words are becoming dynamite…

LILI hangs up nappies.

What are these?

LILI: 'Kak-cloths' the girls call them.

MAYAKOVSKY: What girls?

LILI: At the bicycle factory. I run the nursery there, for the women workers.

MAYAKOVSKY: Lilichka… You practice what you preach.

LILI: Don't you?

MAYAKOVSKY: I don't preach. I write stormography.

LILI: Most of the women down there can't read. They work morning, noon and night. Their faces are like slept-in sheets. When their shift's over, they go home, cook the old man's tea, wash, put the kids to bed, and next day they do it all over again.

MAYAKOVSKY: How do they get on with you?

LILI: The children are wonderful. I teach them painting, and dancing…and they teach me how to play, and laugh, and be alive…

MAYAKOVSKY: I meant the mothers…

LILI: They probably think I'm mad, or a martyr to the revolution…which is a word that means little to most of them. Their husbands killed the Tsar. Most of them could happily throttle their husbands. I try to persuade them to get involved, but like so many people, they're afraid. To commit.

LILI looks at MAYAKOVSKY

MAYAKOVSKY: I was invited to join the Workers Committee on my street. A bunch of plums. The chairman, Sverdlov, is a heap that's become a mountain, a man of real bottom. Alexandria Treblenko, the Secretary, works in the Cannery. A gattling gob, who gossips worse than a man. But ask her a serious question – a fog descends. How they got there, nobody knows. Just turtles washed up by the tide. Bolsheviks… People look at them like deaf men look at people dancing, and think: they're insane.

LILI: Keep talking like that and they'll send you to Astrakhan to catch fish.

MAYAKOVSKY: No. It'll be the lunatic asylum for me. Can you keep a secret, Lili? I suffer from hallucinations. In my mind, I can see, coming, over the mountains of time, that which nobody else has seen. An age when the spaceships of the commune will hurtle out to the moon and the distant planets and teach them that 'we' can be as tender a word as 'me'.

LILI: A beautiful thought.

MAYAKOVSKY: 'Revolution' should be given a new name. A name like lovers give each other on their first night together. When the rivers of the world splash honey, and pave the streets with stars.

LILI: You're a romantic, Volya.

MAYAKOVSKY: Not at all. You've read Marx, in your study group. You and Osip. Love is the motor of history. Without love, for one another, we have no reason to better ourselves or the world.

LILI: I don't recall Marx saying that.

MAYAKOVSKY: But he knew it. Love is the heart of everything. It drives all my belief.

LILI: Yes...

MAYAKOVSKY: Though I doubt Osip would agree with me. He's a calculating, Kipling cat.

LILI: So are our enemies, Volya. That's Osip's concern. Right now, all over Moscow *they* are sitting around samovars, planning, plotting, how to pick the meat out of this stew. That's why he's forming the Left Front for Art, against the philistines. You should be part of that.

39

MAYAKOVSKY: I'm a poet. Just words. Whatever happens, the moon goes on chucking her silver, into the ocean beneath.

LILI: People like you, and me, are despised and feared on all sides. We're 'dilettantes', with fingernails, and soft palms.

MAYAKOVSKY: I am a peasant, Lili. One of the unlanded gentry by birth. I grew up in a chestnut log cabin in the forests of Bagdadi. Where they grow fat grapes. As a child I crawled into the wine barrels, and echoed nursery rhymes, at the top of my voice, as far as the moon. I have a right to moving lips.

LILI: I am afraid for you. That's all.

Pause.

MAYAKOVSKY: You have beautiful eyes, Lili. Black as the pips of a pear.

Music.

If I was destined to be a tsar
On the sunny gold of my coins
I'd order my people:
Mint
Your precious face!
And there
Where the world has faded into tundra
Where the river trades with the North wind
There I'd scratch Lili's name on my chain
And in the darkness of hard labour
Kiss it again and again, and again…

LILI: (*Sings.*) Again and again and again…

MAYAKOVSKY kisses her.
They dance together.
Music segues into:

Scene Five

TITLES: 'kiss and kiss and kiss'
Enter MAYAKOVSKY and LILI, laughing.
The music ends.
OSIP reading, editing poems.

OSIP: Did you miss the tram?

LILI: They weren't running…

MAYAKOVSKY: *You,* on the other hand, missed a treat.
   The Arts club was packed with proletkult noodles.
   Poetry stuck together with spit. Painting done by
   donkeys, with their tails. I read, they sat, silent, covered
   in snow. And Lili did a dance class.

LILI: It was like teaching pigs to waltz.

   OSIP is silent.

   What is it Olya? What's happened?

OSIP: (*To MAYAKOVSKY.*) I presume I was intended to
   read this poem? It was amongst those you handed me…

   MAYAKOVSKY is silent.

LILI: What poem?

   The music quietly underscores.

OSIP: (*Reads.*) There I'd scratch LILI's name on my chain
   And in the darkness of hard labour
   Kiss it again and again, and again…

   The music stops.

LILI: Volodya!?

MAYAKOVSKY: He had to know sometime.

LILI: You did this deliberately!

MAYAKOVSKY: What difference does it make?

LILI: Earth and sky difference!

OSIP: You have slept with him, I presume?

LILI: Yes. I didn't tell you because…

OSIP: How long has this secret liaison been going on?

LILI: Not 'secret', Olya…

OSIP: You just couldn't find the right time to tell me, is that it?

LILI: There is never a 'right time' to speak about these things… I wasn't sure.

MAYAKOVSKY: (*Paranoid.*) Sure of what?

LILI: Myself.

MAYAKOVSKY turns to OSIP.

MAYAKOVSKY: I love her. I will be with her, for her, always…

OSIP: You…are ridiculous…

MAYAKOVSKY: I speak my feelings…

OSIP: Uh! You undress them, like a child flings off its nightgown in front of the fire…

MAYAKOVSKY: In me, it's my soul that goes naked, before an inextinguishable bonfire of inconceivable love for her! (*To LILI.*) Tell him! It's over…finished!

LILI: No…

MAYAKOVSKY: What?

LILI is silent. Then:

LILI: (*To MAYAKOVSKY.*) I'll never abandon Olya…I love him as my lifelong friend, my comrade, and I love you…

MAYAKOVSKY: Impossible!? That cannot be!!

LILI: Calm down! It is possible to love two people, Volodya…three…more… But each differently…

OSIP: You are 'romantic', Lili. More a child than he is!!

LILI: (*Angry.*) Don't speak to me like that!!

OSIP: I speak as your husband…

LILI: On the day I married you, Osip, I said to myself always look at him and say at any moment he could love another…and that way I have kept my love for you alive. There is no contract between us, no marriage that gives you the right to control how I love, or who, or when.

OSIP: (*Sardonic/bitter.*) I wished you only to persuade him, not crawl into bed with him.

MAYAKOVSKY: What does that mean?

OSIP: You'd better ask her.

LILI: Ignore him…

MAYAKOVSKY: Persuade me of what!!??

LILI: He is being destructive, and jealous…

OSIP: Nonsense!!

MAYAKOVSKY: Lili!? I demand to know!!

LILI: Stop it! Stop it!! Both of you!!

There is silence: The three of them angry, jealous, paranoid.

LILI: Jealousy is a false feeling…

OSIP: … I am not jealous…

LILI: … An abominable feeling. A phenomenon of the existing order of things. Of the habit of regarding one's companion as an object to be appropriated. An

43

insatiable thief that destroys our souls. (*To OSIP.*) Isn't it!? Well, isn't it?

OSIP: (*He knows this.*) Yes...

MAYAKOVSKY: I thought you were mine? I am yours completely...

LILI: Volya...I grew up in a bourgeois family, that was a hot little hell, of possession and power. My mother abased herself to my father, who was a...domestic Tsar, who ruled all of us by a divine right which nobody dared to question. Until the revolution, when we turned our backs on all of that, for something different... Didn't we? To love, but to belong to no one, but myself... And I do love you, Volya...

MAYAKOVSKY: Then tell him it is finished!?

LILI: Are you listening to me? Either of you?

OSIP: Yes. I have heard you.

Silence.

What is it you propose? What is to be done?

MAYAKOVSKY: How can you just sit there?

OSIP: Would you prefer it if I spat rage? Turned myself inside out!?

MAYAKOVSKY: Are you capable of that?

LILI: Volodya!

MAYAKOVSKY: Where are his feelings!? (*To OSIP.*) At least curse me! Slap my face...

OSIP: There is no blame in the consequence of a fact, if it is a fact.

MAYAKOVSKY: So cold... You reason...calculate, strangle the life out of everything!

OSIP: No… A match is cold. The tinderbox we strike it on is cold. But the fire that nourishes and warms us springs from them. My 'reason' is only as cold as that.

MAYAKOVSKY: How can you calculate feelings?

OSIP: Before the match is struck. Like you, before you put pen to paper. Before we turn the world upside down and propose a new millennium. We calculate. Because we know our own self-interest is bound up with the interests of everyone else.

LILI: We change nothing if we can't change ourselves… That is the revolution…

MAYAKOVSKY: We're not Commissars, discussing the rationing of bread! This is not politics. This is love!

LILI: 'The heart of everything'…?

MAYAKOVSKY: (*Angrily frustrated.*) I'm not like you! Either of you…

LILI: Volodya…

MAYAKOVSKY: I am what I am!.

LILI: Nonsense. You might as well say art is what it has always been. Put yourself in a museum.

Pause.

LILI: Out there…150 million people are struggling to share the profits of their work, the crops in their fields, the houses in every street. In the midst of all that, we call ourselves 'revolutionaries'… And yet in our petty domestic lives we can't even… How can we be communist with our ideas, and be bourgeois, possessive, about each other!?

Silence.

OSIP: We cannot…

Pause.

LILI: There will have to be arrangements.

MAYAKOVSKY: About what?

LILI: About this.

MAYAKOVSKY: Love is the bidding of the heart not an
act of will to be organised with 'arrangements'.

LILI: (*Firmly.*) I love you, Volya. But, either it is over
between us now or…!

OSIP: Or… We live together…as comrades. (*To
MAYAKOVSKY.*) You could move into the apartment.

MAYAKOVSKY: No…

LILI: Why not?

OSIP: Lili could have the bedroom. I have a divan in my
study. You would have the attic. Those rooms would be
private, no one to enter them without knocking. The
sitting room to be for all, to come and go as we please.
It would be possible…

MAYAKOVSKY: I could not bear it…

OSIP: She is right. We must commit our whole selves to
the revolution, to change in everything, or we change
nothing. (*Beat.*) Volya…You have been an adolescent
long enough. Move in… Join us. Join the Left Front for
Art.

MAYAKOVSKY: (*Suddenly.*) Why don't you just let her
go!?

LILI: He has no hold over me. No one does. I love you,
Volya. We all know the past was what mankind should
not have been. The present is what mankind ought not
to be. The future is…us. We three. Here. (*Pause.*) Kiss,
and kiss, and kiss.

Music.

Scene Six

TITLES: 'the nooses at noon are too tight'
MAYAKOVSKY paces silently reciting a poem.
ANNUSHKA enters she looks under a table. An empty mousetrap.

ANNUSHKA: Damn he's done it again. Woofed the bait without even springing the trap. I'm feeding the little bugger!

MAYAKOVSKY in his own world sits at the table and scribbles a thought down. ANNUSHKA has taken a piece of bread from her pocket, spits on it and rolls it into a ball, as:

MAYAKOVSKY: He's a hero. Would you risk your life to eat?

ANNUSHKA: Do you want mouse shit in our soup? That's the question!

As ANNUSHKA baits the trap.

MAYAKOVSKY: Is it still snowing out there?

ANNUSHKA: The river's iced over. The workers are really walking on water now. And all the damn toilets are frozen.

MAYAKOVSKY: Weather like this you envy the dogs. They can pee in the street without shame.

ANNUSHKA sets the trap.

ANNUSHKA: You'll need to be careful before you go putting your feet under this table. (*Beat.*) You going to be staying long?

MAYAKOVSKY: For always…

ANNUSHKA: We're already houseful.

MAYAKOVSKY: I have nowhere to go. You can't build new houses in winter. I'd make an igloo, but I don't know how.

ANNUSHKA: Save that sort of talk for your scribblings.

MAYAKOVSKY: My scribblings? Have you read my work?

ANNUSHKA: I can't read. Madame Lili's read some of your stuff to me.

MAYAKOVSKY: And…

ANNUSHKA: I think you should write less and say more. That… 'Cloud in Trousers'… What's that when it's at home?

MAYAKOVSKY: It's a metaphor.

ANNUSHKA: What's a metaphor?

MAYAKOVSKY: … A way of saying one thing and meaning several.

ANNUSHKA: Like a riddle? To muddle up people's minds?

MAYAKOVSKY: To make things clearer.

ANNUSHKA: A cloud in trousers? The world's full of enough windy rubbish. There's a ton of manure for every pound of your carrots.

MAYAKOVSKY: Ah… That's a metaphor.

ANNUSHKA: No. It's the truth.

Pause.

MAYAKOVSKY: How long have you known Osip?

ANNUSHKA: Since God was a boy. He's always been decent with me. As my Alexei says: A good employer is water in the desert. But, Master Osip's craftier than that mouse. Sees a chance coming before it's round the corner. Been a Communist since his balls dropped. If the Bolsheviks cut his legs off, he'd say he preferred walking that way.

MAYAKOVSKY: And Lili?

ANNUSHKA: I was her nursemaid. Once we had a lovely apartment. Their wedding dowry was 30,000 roubles. Their parents fled the pogroms. Lili and Osip stayed, married, and gave their place to a Housing Charity, and we came to live in this box. (*Pause.*) Don't think you're the first.

MAYAKOVSKY: First what?

ANNUSHKA: Tobinson, Greshkov... Oh, there's been others:

MAYAKOVSKY: Moved in here?

ANNUSHKA: No... But they all got their shoes under her bed. One road or another. (*Beat.*) Put it like this: Madame Lili's always well turned out, regular baths, oils her skin. She's not taking good care of herself just so her husband can recognise her in the next world.

MAYAKOVSKY: Annushka!

ANNUSHKA: She's as bright as a button, always was. Top of her class at the School of Architecture... A driven, passionate little soul who needs protecting from herself. At fifteen, she decided Osip was going to be her husband.

MAYAKOVSKY: They were childhood sweethearts?

ANNUSHKA: No. It was mainly because her father disapproved of him. You've got a lot to learn, Mr Mayakovsky. The harder it is to get, the more a woman, like Madame Lili, wants it. The easier it comes, the sooner it goes.

Enter LILI.
Exit ANNUSHKA.
MAYAKOVSKY watches as LILI brushes out her hair.
Music.

MAYAKOVSKY: Were you with him last night?

LILI: No…

MAYAKOVSKY: Then why didn't you come to me?

LILI: I wanted to be alone…

MAYAKOVSKY: I was so cold, Lili. My pillow an ice floe. Me a polar bear. Water, where from, and why so much? Myself. Crying, cry baby fool. Water behind the sofa, under the table, and the wardrobe, turning over and over. The bed afloat. Water chilling my feet. A suitcase floats out of the window. Then me, polar bear, on my iceberg pillow, swept along the goose-skinned river, under a bridge. A man stood on the bridge's rail. He began to shout, a booming shout that couldn't be out-shouted: 'Help. Help. Help!' And his voice was mine.

The music ends.

LILI: Volodya… Look at me.

MAYAKOVSKY: No! If you touch me with your eyes, I will explode. You *were* with him! The truth! (*Pause.*) You sit there silent while floor after floor collapses through the raging inferno of my body.

LILI: Stop it! It's too much. Everything with you!

MAYAKOVSKY: If you loved as I love you would murder love. I can't talk it away, eat, drink, write it away. (*Beat.*) Lili… Your eyes are full of blossom. Like two fresh meadows. I just want to tumble around in them, a happy boy. Love me Lili. Love me.

LILI: I do! But don't batter and besiege me like this!

MAYAKOVSKY: Something is happening inside of me. I feel too small for myself. I can't carry a piano. How can I carry this heart of mine?

LILI: Volodya…

MAYAKOVSKY: It's hard for me…

LILI: And me… Free doesn't mean easy…

Pause.

MAYAKOVSKY: I'm frightened, Lili… I was searching for you. The soul no one had seen. In order to put your healing flowers into the wounds of my lips.

Music (of their dance).

Love me, Lili. Don't ever abandon me.

LILI: Always… I will be here for you. Always.

The music ends.

What are you writing? (*Picks up manuscript.*)

MAYAKOVSKY: Osip has got me a commission. From the Ministry of Enlightenment. A tribute to the steel workers of Kursk! It's dross. A poem in praise of scrap iron.

LILI: (*Reading.*) It's good…

MAYAKOVSKY: It's driving me insane. I've re-written it a hundred times for him. I sweat for a poetic phrase, he hacks it down. He'd pluck the tailfeathers from a peacock and send it wooing with a bare arse.

LILI: He knows what he's doing, Volya.

MAYAKOVSKY: He's *not* doing it! I am!! (*Pause.*) At least it pays well. I am now a very proletarian poet. Paid by the line! (*Beat.*) Let's go out dancing tonight!

LILI: It's Wednesday…

MAYAKOVSKY: Oh… Yes…of course. Wednesday is Osip day.

LILI: Don't start again, please.

MAYAKOVSKY: I know… I know… Changing things causes difficulty.

LILI: Tomorrow… We'll do it tomorrow. Drink vodka with the Komsomol youth and dance and make love…

Music:

MAYAKOVSKY:
You wouldn't understand
Why
Cold as an ominous sneer
I am carrying my soul to be slaughtered
For the dinner of the coming years.
I am probably the last poet.
A slave's been kissed into your hearts.
I am dauntless
With a soul strung as the nerves of a wire
I am the lord of electric bulbs.
Come all to me
Those who loom through darkness
Who groan
Because the nooses at noon are too tight
I'll show you
With words simple as mooing
Our new souls
I'll touch your foreheads with my fingers
And you'll grow lips
For enormous kisses
And a tongue
Native to all peoples
Then leaning on my limping soul
I'll stagger towards my throne
With the holes of stars above its tatty dome.
Consoled in soiled clothes,

I'll relax on the soft bedding of my outpourings
And gently kissing the knees of the railroad
The wheel of a locomotive will squeeze my throat.

The music stops.

Scene Seven

TITLE: 'the music of a million cranes'
LILI sketches, MAYAKOVSKY writes.
Enter OSIP with leaflets.

OSIP: Have you seen these!? They're all over Moscow.
(*Reads.*) 'Mayakovsky is a gabbler'… His words are
'chaff, blown on his own wind'. You are 'rotten as a six
month egg', Volodya!

MAYAKOVSKY: Who says that?!

OSIP: Polonsky…

MAYAKOVSKY: That lard arse! I hope his next shit's a
hedgehog!

OSIP: The Proletcults are sharpening their knives for you.

MAYAKOVSKY: I don't give a fish's tit about those
literary gossips and their word-washing quarrels.

OSIP: This is not a quarrel. It's a declaration of war
against us. We must get out a response. A counter blast.

MAYAKOVSKY: 'War'? Polonsky and his rabble have all
the dash of a dismounted cavalry regiment. They have
no poets.

OSIP: Yesenin is becoming popular.

MAYAKOVSKY: Yesenin!? With those floppy peasant
boots, and that slicked down hair? He repeats himself
like the patterns on wallpaper: 'Russia is mine,
undoubtedly mine…' All he wants is to take it, and
butter his bread with it. Don't worry about Yesenin. One

day the Cheka will take him down the Lubianka and beat him to death with his own poems.

OSIP: Ha! (*OSIP makes notes.*) Good… Yes. Now… Here they accuse you and the Left Front of denying the Classics…of being literary hooligans.

MAYAKOVSKY: Let's tell them we are! The Classics have their place. The past. They shouldn't stick their bronze arse in the way of the Future.

LILI: Lenin loves the classics. He's for ever quoting Pushkin.

MAYAKOVSKY: Lenin will never censor us.

OSIP: Don't be too sure. He is a dialectician. A strategist of the mind, suspicious of anything driven by emotionality.

MAYAKOVSKY: No… That's you Osip! The tsar executed Lenin's brother. And that tears at his gut. Lenin is a man driven by love, anger and loss. Ideas are never enough.

OSIP: When will you root out this romanticism. Our great leaders are not men like you. They come from a different place.

MAYAKOVSKY: Where? Where do you think I come from, Olya?

OSIP: Insolent Bohemia. What Comrade Trotsky calls anarchist individualism. He thinks you make too much noise about yourself.

MAYAKOVSKY: What else should a poet do? Is it self-centred to think for one's self? Anyone who doesn't, doesn't think at all. Right?

OSIP is silent.

LILI: (*Smiles.*) Yes, Volodya… You are right.

OSIP: So… How do we respond, about Pushkin and the Classics?

MAYAKOVSKY: Pushkin wrote: 'Set fire to hearts with your words'. We are building bonfires! The Lyricists are writing poetry only their wives want to read. They're still smelling roses. We are inventing them.

OSIP: Good! (*Writes.*)

LILI: You mean to print all this? Say these things in public?

OSIP: We are in a battle, Lili. To the death. Words are the only weapons we have.

MAYAKOVSKY: I'm an arms manufacturer, now. An Explosive Factory of words.

LILI: Be careful, Osya.

OSIP: Of course… I have enough… (*Pause.*) Have you finished the Kursk poem, Volodya?

MAYAKOVSKY: I think so…

OSIP: Excellent. The tour is organised. You will go first to the steel works at Kursk, then three weeks on the road.

MAYAKOVSKY: I thought it was to be published?

OSIP: It will be. But when half the world, the best half, can't read, a poet needs a larynx, not paper.

MAYAKOVSKY: Three weeks? Come with me Lili.

LILI: I can't. Osip and I have work to do here…

MAYAKOVSKY: Is this to be the arrangement? I'm sent to the blast furnaces, while you two stay here, with each other, fireside cosy?

OSIP: What is this?

MAYAKOVSKY: To recite poetry to furnacemen! Stand there like a man at the wrong end of a coconut shy! Your loud speaker in chief!

LILI: That's unfair Volodya.

OSIP: You are a great artist, which I will never be. I've criticised your work, suggested, advised… Nothing more. We are Futurists, Volya, and living in the future is difficult. No easy praise from vulgar minds, and suburban intellects. But you have genius. Believe in it. The workers of Kursk will love you because you speak their hearts, their dreams, their revolution, in words simple as bread. Powerful as fire!

LILI: There has to be trust between us, Volya. We will be here when you return. And we will love you while you are away. Always love you…

OSIP: We are each committed to one another.

MAYAKOVSKY: 'Quiet! You will be quiet! Quiet like flowers'.

Music underscores:

To The Workers of Kursk Who Extracted The First Ore.
From the time
When
Our rhinoceros great grandmothers
Our lizard great great grandfathers and crocodiles
Resembling nothing at all imaginable
Rolled along like ice iron clad…
From the times
Which
Split ferns into layers
And
Hardened
As coal
Iron ore deposits
were laid down.
The hum of machinery
Of future times
Lay
In a stone bag

And not a squeak.
By the music
Of a million cranes
Kursk
Rattles and clicks.
Fiery lipped
Hearths of blast furnaces sigh
Scattering
The stars of outpourings.
On a hundred freight and
Passenger lines
Planes
Set out
Brand new
Flashing
Their aluminium
In the sun.
Cars and engines
Pass in stream.
From wharves
A mile long
Slip into the water.
Ships
For surface
And underwater voyages.
You worked
You fell asleep
You're only a city
Not Shakespeare.
No long-tongued lecturer
Will heap praises
On you
On your anniversary
In the interval of the opera
Or operetta.
The tractor
Will sound forth
About you –

The most convincing electrolecturer.
A million chimneys
Will write
The outline of your names.
The doors of fame
Are narrow doors
But however narrow they may be
You
Will always enter
Who in Kursk
Extracted
Pieces of iron.

The music finishes.

End of Act One

ACT TWO

Scene Eight

TITLE: '1924'
Music.
TITLE: 'a communist polar bear'
Colour wash drawings, hung on the nappy line, to dry.
The music segues into the phone theme.
OSIP is on the phone.

OSIP: If you arrest Mandelstaum, it will make a martyr of
    him… His poetry is indeed self-indulgent. But…some
    seeds you can look at, and know exactly what fruit they
    will bear. Mandelstaum is hardly a 'socially dangerous'
    person… If the Commissar thinks fit, of course, but,
    please, Comrade, ask him to call me…… Thank you,
    Comrade. I'll be here the rest of the day.

> *LILI has entered and overheard the end of the conversation.*
> *The music stops.*
> *LILI takes off her overcoat, pale.*

LILI: The Cheka, again?

OSIP: Just some literary business.

LILI: You promised to have no more to do with them. Now
    all these calls…

OSIP: Things have changed, Lili. Lenin is seriously ill.
    Stalin is poised to slither upwards. He's a toad,
    surrounded by toadyites. Soon all power will be in his
    hands, God knows what's in his mind.

LILI: But them?

OSIP: We need allies, whoever they are. Even if we have to
    feed with the panthers. Poetry is a serious business in
    Russia, now. And we know that, Lili, because they are
    shooting people for it!

LILI: Have you discussed this with Volodya?

OSIP: He doesn't need to know. He is an idealist. He won't understand.

LILI: You make me complicit in your silence!

LILI is momentarily dizzy, and sits.

OSIP: What is it?

LILI: I'm fine… I saw the doctor this morning. He confirmed the pregnancy…

OSIP: I see…

LILI: I had decided before seeing him…

OSIP: And?

LILI: He did it there and then.

Pause.

OSIP: It is for the best. Now is not a good time.

LILI picks up a sketch pad and begins to work on a drawing.

But you should lie down… Rest.

LILI: These have to be finished, today.

LILI sketches. OSIP approaches

OSIP: Do you intend to tell Volodya, of this?

LILI: Yes…

OSIP: Why, Lili? It will merely add his suffering to yours. Some things *are* best left unspoken.

LILI: 'No secrets', you said, Osip. 'No secrets, between comrades'?

Pause.

OSIP: They will be calling me back. I'll take it in my room.

Music.
OSIP goes.
LILI is alone

LILI: (*Sings.*) I'll take my heart
    Wrapped in tears of pain
    And carry it
    Like a dog
    Who drags
    To his kennel home
    A paw run over by a train
    Almighty! A pair of hands you invented
    Arranged for everyone
    A head like this
    Why didn't you see to it
    That without being in pain tormented
    We could
    Kiss and kiss and kiss…

The music ends.
Enter MAYAKOVSKY, pulling off his jacket, enthusiastic.

MAYAKOVSKY: Sorry… There was an incident on the
    Kuznetsky. A horse came a cropper, on the ice.
    Everybody laughed. I cried.

LILI smiles.
MAYAKOVSKY picks up a list.

Let's get cracking… 'Condoms'?! Condoms! What the
    fuck rhymes with condom!!?

LILI: 'One on'…

MAYAKOVSKY: Nah…

LILI painting a sketch with colour wash.

LILI: Musselprom?

MAYAKOVSKY: No… I want that for light bulbs… Big
    picture of a light bulb, sun rays… Under:

'For a sun to shine all day long
Buy your bulbs from Musselprom' .

LILI writes, sketches, as MAYAKOVSKY checks a list:

Babies' dummies…

LILI: (*As she works.*) Tummy…? Mummy…?
Gummy?

MAYAKOVSKY: No… This: Picture…Old man sucking
dummy. Under:

'The best dummies ever sold
he will suck them till he gets old'

LILI: Yes…!

She works. MAYAKOVSKY paces.

MAYAKOVSKY: Another word for condoms?

LILI: Sheaths…? Prophylactics.?

MAYAKOVSKY: Prophylactics! Wonderful word!

Ha…: 'Our prophylactics could save the revolution
If every apparatchik was forced to use one.'

LILI: That'll get you shot!

MAYAKOVSKY: Sometimes the heart yearns for a shot,
the throat for a razor.

LILI: Don't play with such words…

MAYAKOVSKY: I'm not playing with words, I'm playing
with my life.

Pause.

LILI: Volya, there's something…

MAYAKOVSKY: … Ahaah… Draw a picture of
Chekhov…

LILI: Chekhov…?

MAYAKOVSKY: And underneath:

'Ding dong…ding dong
Uncle Vanya's bought a condom.'

LILI smiles, and scribbles.
Enter ANNUSHKA with a basket of washed nappies.
ANNUSHKA picks up one of LILI's sketches.

ANNUSHKA: How much are these?

MAYAKOVSKY: The State pays me 2 roubles for each advert.

ANNUSHKA: I meant the light bulbs.

MAYAKOVSKY: They're cheap. And since there are no others, they're the best.

ANNUSHKA: They're good, the Musselprom stores. I'll give you that.

MAYAKOVSKY: Mass production. Everything 'made by the people, for the people'. The people's lightbulbs shine in every living room. We are the planet's new decorators. Heaven on earth, Annushka!

ANNUSHKA looking at another sketch laughs

ANNUSHKA: Ha ha. That's good! 'Suck it till he gets old.' My Alexei could do with one of these in his gob.

MAYAKOVSKY: So now you appreciate my poetry?

ANNUSHKA: Yes. This is good. You're earning. That's bread on the table.

MAYAKOVSKY has picked up the list of jobs.

MAYAKOVSKY: 'Moscow seamstresses'…

ANNUSHKA: (*To LILI.*) Oh they're good, aren't they? (*To MAYAKOVSKY.*) Lili's bought dresses at Moscow seamstresses.

MAYAKOVSKY: Say that again…

ANNUSHKA: Madame Lili's bought dresses at Moscow seamstresses.

MAYAKOVSKY: Wonderful. (*Writes.*) 'Buy your dresses, at Moscow Seamstresses'.

ANNUSHKA: You're writing that down?

LILI: It rhymes, Annushka.

ANNUSHKA: Oh… Yes. (*Beat.*) I'm a poet and don't know it!

MAYAKOVSKY: We're all poets now.

ANNUSHKA: Do I get 2 roubles?

MAYAKOVSKY: One…

ANNUSHKA: Done. This is money for old rope.

MAYAKOVSKY: It is useful art.

LILI grimaces with pain.

ANNUSHKA: Is your chest bad again?

LILI: No…

ANNUSHKA: You look pasty to me…

LILI: I'm just a little tired…

Music.
The phone rings.
ANNUSHKA moves to answer.

Leave it Annushka…

ANNUSHKA looks at LILI, then goes.

MAYAKOVSKY: What are these phone calls he's been getting lately? Is it a woman? Is Olya having a secret affair?

LILI: No… Volodya… Don't…

MAYAKOVSKY gently lifts the phone, gesturing her to be quiet. He listens intently.
He puts down the phone.

It's not what you think.

MAYAKOVSKY: What I 'think'? You too? Can you tell what people are thinking, just by looking at them? They say the Cheka can see into people's brains like they're looking at a watch with its back off. (*Pause.*) What the hell is going on!!

LILI silent.
Enter OSIP. He picks up his hat about to go.

OSIP: I'll be out for supper…

MAYAKOVSKY: Singing for it at the Lubianka?

OSIP looks at LILI.

LILI: He listened in…

MAYAKOVSKY: I didn't know you had friends there?

OSIP: I do work for them sometimes. Drafting papers, articles…

MAYAKOVSKY: For the nocturnal diplomats? They have blood on their hands.

OSIP: They are a necessary evil.

MAYAKOVSKY: They're a parcel of slippery turds!

LILI: Be calm, Volodya.

OSIP: Listen to me… After October, the whites, the armies of intervention, swarmed here, to strangle all this at birth. There were saboteurs amongst us, opportunists everywhere. You know that as well as I do. They had to be rooted out. No mercy.

MAYAKOVSKY: That was Civil War. This is the Age of the Commune. And the Cheka are still spiriting people away to their corrective camps… Some of them writers.

OSIP: Yes…

MAYAKOVSKY: Writers we have ridiculed, publicly rubbished. Joked about sending to the Lubianka! I despised them. I hated their petty scribblings, but I would never, ever send a man to prison, to his death, for what he wrote!!

OSIP: Nor me.

MAYAKOVSKY: Swear it Osip! On your love for me. Promise me, we have not been doing the Cheka's dirty work.

OSIP: I swear Volodya. No.

MAYAKOVSKY: Then why do you associate with them!? Why do you deal with a closed shop where the merchandise is death?

OSIP: Because I fear, one day, I may have an account there. We both might.

MAYAKOVSKY: No. I joined with you, the Left Front for Art! Not the Party! I'm free to speak my mind, whatever flag flies over the damn Kremlin.

OSIP: And that is why they don't trust you. I have worked alongside them to protect you. It had to be done…

LILI: Osip's right.

MAYAKOVSKY: The people trust me. They know where my heart is, and who, and what, it is for. That's all the protection I need.

OSIP: We've walked a tightrope with Lenin. He's tolerated us, taken us half way there. Now the wire has tightened. We don't live in the world we are striving for, Volya.

Even Trotsky could fall. History is made by such accidents.

MAYAKOVSKY: Says who!

OSIP: Marx… Revolution is a leap into the open air of history. Tsarism fell apart on us. The old civilisation destroyed itself. And one day, Capitalism, the posturing peacock of the West will disintegrate. Their world will become a glittering heap of trash, made by machines, that the redundant workers, wageless, cannot afford to buy. And what follows all such events, there, as here, is either barbarism or the triumph of revolution. And both are always bloody.

MAYAKOVSKY: Perhaps I should come with you to the Cheka now?

OSIP: That's not funny.

MAYAKOVSKY: Oh… Don't worry, Olya. The Cheka can torture me all they like, I'll never give evidence against Stalin. I'll rustle in their hands and tell them I'm only paper.

OSIP: Your poetry has been an army nobody can make march to their order. And it has to go on marching.

MAYAKOVSKY: Where? Where are we marching, Olya?

OSIP: To the future. Where else is there?

Music.
Exit OSIP.
Music underscores:

MAYAKOVSKY:
So… I want to weep unrestrained
A communist polar bear.
But with all my breathing, heart beating
Voice rending
With every hair's bristle in spiked terror upending

With the holes of my nostrils
The nails of my eyes
With my teeth set on edge in bestial cries
With my brows angry muster
My porcupining skin, with a trillion pores
Literally, each pore wide
Awake, asleep, I accept not
I hate, all of it, everything
Everything into us past slavishness drives
Everything that in swarming trifles team
Ossifying and assifying living
Even in our own Red flag society.

Pause.

I feel like a machinist with his sleeve caught in the cogs, drawn in, already surrendered to inevitability… and there is no heaven.

Music:

LILI: (*Text into song.*) There is… You have described it: the horizontal line of the sea, undisturbed, even in bad weather, by the beating of waves or the spume of a passing squall… That order and peace is the heaven we exist for… Nothing more. And I feel that existence, always, beating in my wrists…

The music ends.

MAYAKOVSKY: Is this my debt to the universe? Always paying a percentage in pain?

LILI: Isn't great writing always a response to pain? (*Pause.*) You must trust Osip.

MAYAKOVSKY: Why? He clearly doesn't trust me.

LILI: He's doing what he thinks is best. That is the truth.

MAYAKOVSKY: I am not a child Lili. I can face the truth only when I know what it is.

Pause.

LILI: I had to see the doctor today.

MAYAKOVSKY: Are you ill?

LILI: I was pregnant, Volya…

MAYAKOVSKY: Are you sure? Lili! That's wonderful…

LILI: No… No. I saw the doctor to arrange a termination.

MAYAKOVSKY: You can't! No, Lili!

LILI: A child now is impossible… It would be too much work and the disruption of everything …

MAYAKOVSKY: It would be everything to me! I won't let you!

LILI: It is already done! This morning…

Silence.

MAYAKOVSKY: Whose child was it? Mine or Osip's?

LILI: I don't know… I…

MAYAKOVSKY: Whose?!

LILI: Yours…

MAYAKOVSKY: Did you not think to discuss this with me, before…?

LILI: … It had to be my decision.

MAYAKOVSKY: Yours no more than mine, Lili!! Do my feelings mean nothing? I have sacrificed, stifled enough in myself already. Look at me: a jingoist, writing adverts for dummies… Fine! But not this… A man should have children…

LILI: Would you have taken care of it? How?

MAYAKOVSKY: We'd have found a wet nurse. Annushka would have helped…

LILI: No, Volya! *I* was nursed by Annushka. My parents never there for me. I won't do that. I can't.

MAYAKOVSKY: I don't understand you, Lili. You love children. You work in that nursery for next to nothing. Why not children of our own?

LILI: Those kids down there are *all* our own.

MAYAKOVSKY: If two children were standing in the road, one yours, one someone else's, and a runaway cart was hurtling towards them, which one would you save first? Answer me? What would you do?

LILI: I would make sure that no children were ever left in the road, uncared for.

MAYAKOVSKY: You sound like Osip. (*Beat.*) Did you discuss this with him?

LILI: Olya knew… Yes…

MAYAKOVSKY: Then why wasn't I told?!

LILI: Because of this! You rage and you rant and make it impossible for anybody to think straight…

MAYAKOVSKY: Osip persuaded you, didn't he!

LILI: No!! I went to the doctor, and he offered to do it, within the hour… And I knew, in that moment… my mind was made up. It was my decision, alone.

Pause.

MAYAKOVSKY: Children are the flowers of life… Your womb and my seed…

LILI: Yes… But they grow in women, Volodya. The curse of Eve: 'in sorrow shall you bring forth children, and thy desires shall all be to thy husband, and he shall rule over thee'.

MAYAKOVSKY: That's the muttering of priests…

LILI: They *wrote* it! And millions go to church every Sunday and believe it's gospel.

MAYAKOVSKY: I wouldn't be such a husband…

LILI: I'm not offering you the chance.

MAYAKOVSKY: Is that our future, then? Always? Never children?

LILI: Now, in these times… It's what we have chosen.

MAYAKOVSKSY: *I* didn't choose!!

LILI: Yes you did! You and I, and Osip agreed: to love and live together as Comrades, committed to the revolution. Not to live for ourselves, but for a future, Volya…for those kids in the nursery… It wasn't easy for me to make this decision, and your pain is no greater than mine…believe me.

MAYAKOVSKY: I don't know if I can bear it.

LILI: Don't abandon me, Volya. I love you.

Music (the Dance theme.)
Music segues into:

Scene Nine

TITLE: 'the ache that cuts and hacks'
Music underscores:

MAYAKOVSKY:
When I look for the grandest day of my life
Rummaging in all I've gone through and seen,
I name without doubt or internal strife
October 25, 1917.

Brisk, but inconspicuous, Lenin came.
Lenin, drowsy with fatigue, it would seem,
Pacing, stopping, hands clasped behind back,
dug his eyes into the motley scene.
From near, unto far, it went rolling,
mounting from a whisper to a roar:
'Peace to cottages poor and lowly,
war on palaces, war, war, war!'
We fought, in all factories humble and famous
shook 'em out of cities like peas, while outside
the October wildfire left flaming manors
for landmarks, marking its triumphant stride
Fearing no effort or artifice by the rich
on speeds our engine in curling smoke
When suddenly – the shattering news: Ilyich
Had a stroke. It's him they bear from Paveletsky station
through the city that he from the lords released.
The streets like a wound that'll worsen and worsen
So the ache of it cuts and hacks.
Here every cobble knew Lenin in person
by the tramp of the first October attacks.
And from each banner, from every fold
Lenin, alive as ever, cries:
'Workers, prepare for the last assault!
Slaves, unbend your knees and spines!
Proletarian army, rise in force!
Long live the revolution with speedy victory
the greatest and justest of all the wars
Ever fought in history!'

The music ends.

Scene Ten

TITLE: 'a horse on its arse'
MAYAKOVSKY writing. Enter ANNUSHKA. Concealing something behind her back.

ANNUSHKA: Close your eyes.

MAYAKOVSKY closes his eyes.
ANNUSHKA produces a plate on which are slices of bread cheese and butter.

ANNUSHKA: Smell that…

MAYAKOVSKY: Mmm… Cheese! Fresh bread?!

MAYAKOVSKY opens his eyes.

MAYAKOVSKY: And butter. Where did you get it?

ANNUSHKA: The shops are full. The bakers are selling big round loaves, and calling them 'Stalins'. His picture's on every street corner. He's got a face like an owl's arse, but we've food on the plate!

MAYAKOVSKY eats bread and cheese.

MAYAKOVSKY: Mmmm… I love goat's cheese…

ANNUSHKA takes a letter from her pocket, and passes it to MAYAKOVSKY.

ANNUSHKA: I've had this letter come this morning. Looks official.

MAYAKOVSKY opens and reads.

ANNUSHKA: Is it from that Garinsky, him off the Sanitary Committee? Little shit. They should put his name on everybody's lavatory brush.

MAYAKOVSKY: It's not from the Sanitary Committee…

Silence.

ANNUSHKA: It's about Nikolai isn't it?

MAYAKOVSKY: Yes… Shall I read?

ANNUSHKA nods.

(*Reads.*) 'Dear Comrade, It is with great sadness, and pride, that I inform you of the death of your son,

Infantryman Nikolai Tomsky. He fell in action, when the avenging army of the Proletariat was turned upon wreckers and kulak saboteurs, in the black earth province of the Volga. Enemies of the revolution, who were hoarding grain and stocks, while the People starved… His death was an heroic service to the Soviet fatherland…'

Silence.

These are terrible times…

ANNUSHKA: Everything different. Always the same. If it's not meat, it's bones.

MAYAKOVSKY: I'm so sorry, Annushka…

ANNUSHKA: He was a good boy. Straight as two yards of pump water.

MAYAKOVSKY: They say, here, his body will be sent to you in a return coffin.

ANNUSHKA: 'Return'?

MAYAKOVSKY: The body's yours. The box goes back.

ANNUSHKA: Nothing wasted, ey?

MAYAKOVSKY: Nikolai died making history, Annushka. For you, me, all of us. For love… Love of the Commune, like thousands in storming October's heaven fell.

ANNUSHKA: 'Love'? My child is dead. You have to feel that kind of pain, to know, to really know, what love is… *You* lot can make history if you want to… It's as much as I can manage to take care of things on my own doorstep. I want to live in a nice apartment, again, like the one we had on Gorky Prospect, before all this. Where there's cakes, and rolls, and marmalade, tea and chocolate. And nobody's getting shot.

MAYAKOVSKY: Don't lose hope, Nushka… Or my heart
will stop living…

Pause.

Grib
Grab
Grob
Grub.
Wind-drunk
Ice-shod
The street slippery slides.
On its cruppers
A horse came a cropper.
Jeers jingled and capered:
'A horse is down!'
'A horse on its arse!'
Kuznetsky roared with laughter.
Alone I
Didn't join my voice in the general roar.
I went up to him and saw
Equine eyes…
The street slippled over,
Flowing as before…
I went up and saw –
Tear after tear furrow
Down his muzzle,
Hide in his hair…
And some sort of common
Animal sorrow
Poured from me splashing
Running, rustling there.
'Horse don't cry.
Listen to me, horse.
D'you think you're any worse than they?
Dear child,
We're each a bit of a horse, of course,
Everyone's a horse in some sort of way.'
Maybe

The horse was old
And for soothing had no need,
Maybe, for him too trite was my idea, –
Still
the horse
jerked up,
stood on its feet,
then neighed,
and trotting disappeared.
Flicking its tail –
A ginger yearling bold.
Came merrily in,
And stood in the stall.
And it all seemed to him –
That he was a colt
And work was worthwhile,
Life worth living after all!

Music.

Scene Eleven

TITLE: 'the steel of words corrodes'
OSIP at the window. LILI enters.

OSIP: Lili… You see… In the leather coats, there by the black sedan. Those two, puffed out like pigeons.

LILI: Who are they?

OSIP: Shadowmen. They're watching the house…

LILI: Us?

OSIP: Volodya.

LILI: Oh God… Is he in danger?

OSIP: The whisper is that Stalin will shortly issue a decree banning all 'unsuitable words'… If that happens, they may move against Volodya.

LILI: But Stalin loved his Lenin poem. He wept.

OSIP: Crocodile tears. Nobody's safe now, Lili. Give them the man and they'll make the case against him.

LILI: They wouldn't dare arrest Volya.

OSIP: Stalin only wants poetry he can brush his teeth with. That will serve. Volya's work attacks the very philistinism and rot they are building on. Volya must leave.

LILI: Leave?

OSIP: Go abroad. I think I can get him to America.

Pause.

LILI: If Volya goes, I will go with him.

OSIP: You can't.

LILI: Why?

OSIP: Listen to me, Lili! Trotsky has fled. They are not studying Marxism up at the Kremlin anymore, they are studying Zoology. The sheep will finally be separated from the goats. And slaughtered. Trotsky was more than Stalin's rival, he was a Jew, a 'Cosmopolitan'. Like us. We are everything the great man despises…

LILI: October put an end to all of that. People are beyond such animal prejudice.

OSIP: It will never end! To establish an ideology you must create enemies. And who are always the first? Who do they string up from lamp posts when the terror is unleashed? We lived through the pogroms as children. You know this Lili! His association with us damages him.

LILI: I love him.

OSIP: Do you want to love him to death?

Pause.

LILI: Is it really his neck you're worried about, Osip? Or yours?

OSIP: That is a suggestion beneath contempt. If Volya leaves Russia with you: a Jewess, a fellow traveller, another man's wife…there may be no way back for him, or you.

Enter MAYAKOVSKY.

MAYAKOVSKY: Where were you two?!

OSIP: I had a meeting to attend. Lili wasn't well. How was it?

MAYAKOVSKY: The Party philistines came again. A pack of Adams with parted hair. All oaths, beer and stupidity. They booed me to shreds. For the revolution, I have written slogans, adverts, agitprop, become a bloody parrot, and still they accuse me of Individualism.

LILI: How dare they!

MAYAKOVSKY: Because I write 'I': 'I love'. The fucking tsar used to write 'we'! 'We, Nicholas the 2nd, are not amused!' Does that make him a Communist!? Does a Proletcult propose to his sweetheart by saying: '*We* love you'? If he does, she's gonna ask: 'Just how many of you are there?'!

OSIP: This is bad, Volya…

MAYAKOVSKY: Baahh! I'm used to rocks being thrown, this is cotton wool.

OSIP: Don't underestimate them. I've just come from the Ministry of Enlightenment. Stalin has them all trembling. His smile empties the room.

MAYAKOVSKY: Who cares what those spineless 'yesmen' are doing! You fear him? The face that launched a thousand shits!?

OSIP: Yes… So should you.

MAYAKOVSKY: Stalin is a double dealer with a divided soul, whose bedtime reading is reports on the production of pig iron…shall I write *them* next? Or maybe go and sign on at the Hall of Writers! They're issuing rabbits there, these days. Scribblers queue up for their ration. One rabbit for each writer. You can take it home, boil it, dine off it, and wear a rabbit hat on your head for ever afterwards. Go to the National theatre. Everybody's wearing one. It's pathetic!

LILI: Listen to Osip, Volya.

OSIP: I think it would be wise for you to go.

MAYAKOSVSKY: Go? Go where?

OSIP: To America.

MAYAKOVSKY: Don't be ridiculous!

OSIP: We still have a few friends left. I can arrange for you to be appointed official correspondent for *Izvestia*. But you must go now! While a visa can still be got for you.

MAYAKOVSKY: You think Russia will look better from a distance?

LILI:: You will be free…to write. Volodya, you must survive the coming darkness. Beyond the reach of your tormentors.

OSIP: Be an ambassador for us. Send back articles. Expose the West. We will use them to keep your name alive.

MAYAKOVSKY: While they strangle everything we have bled and sweated for!? The clear liquid no longer lies at the bottom of secret cellars, it shines in our glasses and beckons to us.

OSIP: We can't make them drink. Stalin will silence you. Your very life is at stake.

MAYAKOVSKY: Go to America? Heap my poems in a pillow case and sleep on them? Drink bath tub gin and doze in my shirt sleeves? Rather a bullet to my head!

OSIP: It is our duty to survive.

MAYAKOVSKY: They will carve that on your gravestone, Osip. (*Beat.*) Will you come with me?

OSIP: No…

MAYAKOVSKY: I'm asking Lili!

Pause.

LILI: It's best I stay here…

MAYAKOVSKY: No! I cease to exist without you. I won't leave. I can't write without you. You are my family… Is this the love of comrades?!

OSIP: Truly it is.

Pause.

MAYAKOVSKY: (*To LILI.*) Whatever happens… 'Never abandon'… You said!!

LILI: I'm not abandoning you…

MAYAKOVSKY: Then come with me!

LILI: I can't… There is danger in your association with us. Tell him Osip. There are reasons…

MAYAKOVSKY: Osip's reasons, Lili. He blows you like a whistle and you come to heel.

OSIP: You can no longer hide in the forest of your words. The edges are vanishing, the axes are being sharpened.

LILI: Go. Just for a couple of months.

MAYAKOVSKY: Why must I always sacrifice everything? Dreaming, waiting, and terrified I'm standing in the wrong queue.

ANNUSHKA enters.

They're sending me away, Annushka.

ANNUSHKA: Where to?

MAYAKOVSKY: The U.S.A… (*Pause.*) I'll see if cowboys
and Indians really exist. They only want me for a
Commisar's hack here. I'd die if I could but, like they
say… horses rarely commit suicide.

Music.

Whatever happens, I will be here always, like the water
mains run through the streets. (*Beat.*) Will you give me
some 'last tenderness to pave my parting footfalls'?

Music underscores:

I have made myself a soviet factory
Manufacturing happiness.
I don't want to be a wayside flower
Plucked after work in an idle hour.
I want State plan to sweat in debate
Assigning my output as part of the State
I want at the shifts end the factory Committee
To shut my lips with a padlock and key.
I want the pen to equal the gun
To be listed with iron and industry.
Proletarians come to Communism from the depths
      beneath.
The depths of mines, sickles, and factories.
But I from poetry's skies plunged into Communism
Because for me, without it, there is no love.
It's all the same whether I banished myself
Or was sent to hell disdained –
The steel of words corrodes
The brass of brass tarnishes.
Now, beneath foreign rains
Must I soak, rot, and rust?

Music segues into American blues.

Scene Twelve

TITLE: 'as an eskimo stares at a train'
OSIP, LILI and ANNUSHKA. OSIP reads a letter.

MAYAKOVSKY: … The nights are grey, pierced only by
winking eyes on the flashing billboards. I keep
dreaming of Moscow. Blue nights…the snowflakes,
swimming like fish in an aquarium. New York is a giant
accident stumbled upon by children. Streets stand on
end, houses reach to the stars. Skyscrapers, palaces,
hotels, shops… I walk through the richest streets in the
world, but it feels like I am walking amongst ruins.

In the grey mirage of evening
Humbly I step onto Brooklyn Bridge.
So I enveloped in star studded skies
Look at New York, through Brooklyn Bridge.
What pride I take in that steel mile
From it arises a living vision
The struggle for construction, instead of style.
The stern calculus of steel precision.
If this world for us should come to an end
And our planet in chaos, burst into bits
And one thing alone remained of men
This spanning-earth, ruined, uprearing bridge
Then how, as from a tiny needle-thin bone
A museum restores a giant brontosaurus
A centuries-hence geologist from this bridge alone
Could recreate all that now lies before us.
'This very paw of steel' he would say,
'Oceans and prairies united
From here Europe swept to the West far away
Slewed up Indian feathers in airy flight'
He would know by these lines of electric strands
This was the epoch that followed steam.
Here people the skies in aeroplanes spanned
Here people devised the radio beam.
Here life for some was comfort unalloyed

For others a desperate drawn out howl.
From here the hungry unemployed
Into the East river threw themselves down
So I stare as an Eskimo stares at a train
I cling to this like a tick latched on a cat
Yeah... Brooklyn Bridge is something like that!

Scene Thirteen

TITLE: 'wrapped in tears'
ANNUSHKA cleans. LILI reads a letter.
Music underscores:

MAYAKOVSKY: Dear little Puppy, Lilya. I'm sitting in a restaurant, in New York City, howling. The waitresses are laughing at me. It's terrifying to think the rest of my life will be like this... I really must have grown up too much. I know if it has come to an end, I'll be removed like a stone from a stream, and your love will go on washing over all the rest. Don't be ill. I kiss you sunray... I kiss all your sweet places.

The music ends.
LILI suffers a coughing fit.

ANNUSHKA: Let me fetch the doctor to you...

LILI: There's no money left.

ANNUSHKA: We'll pay the doctor with one of Volya's poetry books. Tell him it's 'for internal use only'.

Enter OSIP.

OSIP: Volodya's sent a wire. His visa's nearly run out. He says he's 'constructing a pair of wings to fly home'.

LILI: When?

OSIP: I've cabled him to stay there. I think I can get his visa extended. He must not come back now. Here... he sends you kisses...

LILI takes the telegram and pockets it. She picks up a pair of gloves.

You're not going out? You'll catch your death…

LILI: I have to…

OSIP: Why?

LILI: Tobinson's back in Moscow. He's in a terrible state…

OSIP: No. Oh, Lili! Steer clear of him.

LILI: He's suicidal…

OSIP: And he just called up to let you know that, did he? Misery loves company.

LILI: His wife has left him.

OSIP: I wonder why? The man's a drunkard. Always has been. He's got three children and a liver to support. He doesn't need you.

LILI: I have to go to him.

OSIP: No!

LILI: You don't own me Osip!

Pause..

OSIP: Do what you will.

OSIP goes.
LILI coughing, begins to pull on a glove.

ANNUSHKA: Lilichka.

LILI: Tobinson is desperate…

ANNUSHKA: Suicide is a private matter between a man and his God. Not something you put on a hook and go fishing with…

LILI: He has no one else to turn to.

ANNUSHKA: That's his problem. Why make it yours?

LILI: Because he is a comrade. I can't just shut the door on him. Close my heart to his pain.

ANNUSHKA: You've got enough pots on the boil with your own family.

LILI: I have none. Not like that.

ANNUSHKA: Master Osip? Volodya? They are your family. Look after your own first. It's only human nature.

LILI: What does human 'nature' mean, Annushka? People lived in caves once. Worshipped buffalos. Things change. So can we. There are other ways to be with each other...

ANNUSHKA: And to suffer... You're not happy.

LILI: Are you? With your Alexei?

ANNUSHKA: We get on...

LILI: And love?

ANNUSHKA: We've both passed a lot of water since then. There's many a night I lay there thinking better a single coffin than this double bed. But he tips his wages up and we manage.

LILI: And that's it? Nothing more than that?

ANNUSHKA: The question doesn't come up.

LILI: It has come up. Now. Here. In Russia. Why can't we love more than one person? Open our hearts to one another, family or not?

ANNUSHKA: You live in a different world, Lili.

LILI: I'm trying to...

ANNUSHKA goes. LILI pulls on her glove and goes.

Scene Fourteen

TITLE: 'the clawed bear of jealousy'
MAYAKOVSKY enters the empty apartment, with a suitcase

MAYAKOVSKY: Lili!? Osip!?

> *He takes a bottle of vodka from his pocket. Opens and swigs it.*
> *Enter OSIP.*

Olya! Come let me kiss your little baldness.

> *They embrace.*

Red Star vodka!

> *OSIP refuses the bottle of vodka*

OSIP: Didn't you get my telegrams? I urged you not to return. Not yet!

MAYAKOVSKY: I was so bored there, way out ahead of everyone. Better to die of vodka than boredom. (*Drinks.*) I met this writer, in a bar in Manhattan. A good leftist, pouring his heart out in words. He was truly 'in mourning for his life'. The Americans had their revolution. A different revolution, whose God is freedom, more and more freedom, but they don't know what to do with their damn freedom! And they have a more terrible censorship, in America, than the Kremlin's.

OSIP: What do you mean?

MAYAKOVSKY: When he's surrounded by a culture that is childish and insufficient, a writer censors himself. The West *is* a glittering heap of trash, Olya. A bad taste everywhere. The taste of a public enfeebled with cynical and brutish writings, and movies. I have written an article on all this for *Isvestia*. Over there, art is commercialised and dragged in the mud. It's lost sight of its own destiny.

OSIP: What did they make of you?

MAYAKOVSKY: They loved me. I gave seven readings from the Opera House to Coney Island. Cheered me to the rooftops. We are their inspiration, Osip. That's why I came back. Russia does look better from a distance. Whatever the difficulties, we are the hope of the world.

OSIP: *Izvestia* won't publish anything from you, Volya…

MAYAKOVSKY: Why not?!

OSIP: Things were bad when you left. It's changed since then. It's got worse. The Left Front for Art has collapsed. Pasternak has deserted us.

MAYAKOVSKY: Bollocks to him! When the wind cuts up rough, fair weather ships are the first to turn about.

OSIP: We are completely friendless in the Ministry of Culture. The Commissars are now all art historians in uniform, philistines commissioning statues of bricklayers. Shallow philosophy in deep places everywhere…

MAYAKOVSKY: You are tired, Olya. It's understandable. But I am back with the strength of an elephant. I'm writing a play. *The Bedbug.* About a parasitic louse, Philistinus vulgaris: Pryspkin. A fat cat fool. Marries a pregnant hairdresser. Buys a fur-lined brassiere to make two bonnets in case his wife has twins. Ha! Orders red herrings for his nuptuals. A red wedding. (*Pause.*) And I'm going to put on an Exhibition: everything I've ever written, painted, made… A history of Futurism… You and Lili will help me mount it. Yes?

OSIP: (*Weakly.*) Of course…

MAYAKOVSKY: A celebration of everything into which we have poured our entire souls. We are not finished! To the Future! (*Drinks.*)

Enter LILI.

LILI: Volodya!

They embrace.

OSIP: I have some work to complete. I'm sure you two have much to say to each other. Til this evening.

OSIP goes. LILI coughs.

MAYAKOVSKY: Osip has been neglecting you. He should have brought in a forest of conifers, and set up the sea in your bedroom.

LILI: (*Smiles.*) Yes...

MAYAKOVSKY: What's happening here? He has stolen the eyes of a beaten dog.

LILI: You know Olya. Things are bad. Your room is ready. Everything's just as you left it.

MAYAKOVSKY swigs vodka.

MAYAKOVSKY: I saw your sister on my way through Paris.

LILI: How is Elsa?

MAYAKOVSKY: The same as ever. She goes on painting her 'Still Life'. Knows nothing about what's happening in Moscow, but everything about the latest daubings in every attic in Montmartre.

Pause.

I got your letter. About you and Tobinson. You're still seeing him?

LILI: He's gone back to Leningrad.

MAYAKOVSKY: Just an old flame briefly rekindled, then?

LILI: It wasn't like that.

MAYAKOVSKY: What was it like? Were you fucking him!? Well?? It's not a secret is it? Did you discuss *me* with him? How many times? Was it good? Better than me?

LILI: Please, Volodya…

MAYAKOVSKY: We might as well have the truth. 'Between Comrades'. I know I've never satisfied you. Have I?

LILI: Don't say that…

Pause.

MAYAKOVSKY: Was it here? In this house?

LILI: No! He came to me in trouble.

MAYAKOVSKY: You want my forgiveness? Is that it?

LILI: There's nothing to forgive.

MAYAKOVSKY: No…

LILI is silent.

MAYAKOVSKY: I fell in love in Paris.

LILI: With who?

MAYAKOVSKY: One of our own. A white Russian hiding there. Tatiana…

LILI: What?!

MAYAKOVSKY: We didn't talk politics. You'd like her. Very artistic. Makes hats. Swims, plays tennis, and counts her lovers…

LILI: What number were you?

MAYAKOVSKY: I don't know. (*Beat.*) There was a street trader at the Railway Station, with an alphabet board, selling letters for sticking on wellingtons, to avoid mix-ups. I bought some and sent them to her.

LILI is silent.

You're jealous?!

LILI: No.

MAYAKOVSKY: You are!

LILI: I'm angry! A White Russian. These things are noticed. It will have come back here, and been marked against you.

MAYAKOVSKY: No. Admit it. You are jealous.

LILI: You were free, Volya. Both of us were. We've always said that, from the beginning. None of this changes what we feel for each other.

MAYAKOVSKY: Do you know what I feel? I feel you don't know what love is, Lili. Never have done.

LILI: Are you mocking me?!

MAYAKOVSKY: I mock myself. I once wrote poetry. Magnificent poetry: 'To love is to break away from bedsheets, torn with insomnia, run into the yard and chop wood, all night with a shining axe, with all your strength. Jealous of the moon…' Yes, jealous. I was right! It is all or it is nothing. That is why you are weak. Why you lose hope so easily. Why you sit there and tell me: 'things are bad'. In that whimpering voice.

LILI: Don't Volya!

MAYAKOVSKY: You wanted it to be like this. I gave you everything. Agreed to all that you asked of me… But you? What have you ever sacrificed, Lili? Really given?

LILI: To you? Everything I could, Volya. And my pleasures, fine things, comfort without shame. All that Elsa enjoys in Paris. For a revolution that is now sinking into the mire of male egos and mass stupidity. Don't do this Volya. Don't make love cruel and selfish between us. Not now.

MAYAKOVSKY: It is easy to be cruel in love. When you are half-hearted. I was completely yours! Why is it so wrong? You have tormented me, and tormented yourself. Denied me children. Always denying what you really wanted…

LILI: Is that what you think?

MAYAKOVSKY: I have thought about nothing else, twiddling my toes in Atlantic Cities, sitting on the edge of life, for months and months… Gnawing at my heart. Why? What were you afraid of? Yourself? Of the commitment you and Osip talked so much about, in other things? What?

LILI: Your possessiveness!

MAYAKOVSKY: What do you women want of us!? You have always bounced me around like a ball!!

LILI: Stop shouting! You always run from the hardest things and rage. Out there, you've stood up and shouted, at the top of your voice: 'Wrench the world upside down, Comrades!' And revelled in the applause. Communism in words is easy belief. But change yourself? There are no medals, no applause for that.

MAYAKOVSKY: You think I've given up nothing? Changed nothing in me? I've become a clerk, not a poet. I have committed my soul. I will finish what we began, or they will finish me. I'll write until my only way out of this, my last full stop, is a bullet to my brain.

Exit MAYAKOVSKY.
Music:

LILI opens his suitcase. She finds there a gun. Puts it back.
She picks up a notebook, reads.

LILI: (*Spoken and sung.*)
Life must be changed to begin with
And having changed it – then one can sing.
These days are difficult for the pen.
What great ones ever chose where and when?
A path already trodden, smooth and easy?
The word is the commander in chief of human powers.
Forward march! That time may whistle by like rockets.
Our planet is poorly equipped for delight.
One must snatch gladness from the days that are.
In this life it's not difficult to die.
To make life is more difficult by far.

The music ends.

Scene Fifteen

TITLE: 'the heart of everything'
LILI wrapped up warm. Coughing.
ANNUSHKA decorates a small Christmas tree. She sings to the
tune of 'Tannenbaum'.

ANNUSHKA: (*Unaccompanied.*)
Oh Christmas tree, oh christmas tree
Your branches… (etc.)
Ta da di daa daa dee dee…

The music ends.

LILI: Is it still snowing?

ANNUSHKA: Bitter out. The wind's changed direction.

LILI coughs.

Keep indoors, Lili. (*Pause.*) We'll have a good Christmas
this year.

LILI: Season of good will to all men. We can, at least, all be communists once a year.

ANNUSHKA: Good things are always best kept in the family.

LILI: Annushka…

ANNUSHKA: Isn't this what you wanted? The revolution's coming up trumps. We will have heaven on earth before long.

LILI: I think heaven is a direction, Nushka, not a place. (*Beat.*) What's that?

ANNUSHKA has a picture of Stalin.

ANNUSHKA: Uncle Joe. For the top of the tree. Everybody's doing it this year.

LILI: Not us!

ANNUSHKA: What have you got against him? He's building workers' apartments down by the river. There's no wars, and the price of pigs' meat is steady again. People like to know there's somebody up there, who's in charge. Somebody with a plan. That's why God's popular and so is Stalin.

LILI: He will turn us into the people we warned ourselves against, Nushka.

ANNUSHKA: He's just another one, like the others, come to wet nurse the world. (*Beat.*) I'll put the star up there, then.

LILI picks up a silver star.

LILI: The star of David.

ANNUSHKA: I suppose it is… You forget Christ was a Jew.

LILI: If Christ was alive now, Comrade Stalin would be hosting his last supper.

Enter OSIP.

OSIP: What's this?

ANNUSHKA: Christmas is coming.

OSIP: Christmas?! Christ…a…mess! Remove it, Annushka. Go on… Put it in your own room. It will be better appreciated there.

LILI: Olya?

OSIP: We will not be here for Christmas.

LILI: Not here?

OSIP: We're going South. Where the climate is kinder. For the good of your health, Lili. Take it out, Annushka.

ANNUSHKA goes with the tree

LILI: Osip… I am not going South or anywhere.

OSIP: You will die in this weather.

LILI: What about Volodya? His exhibition opens next week. 'Twenty Years of Work'…

OSIP: He can take care of that himself. I warned him not to come back!

LILI: We have to be there for him.

OSIP: Let it go, Lili. Volodya is saying the things nobody wants to hear now.

LILI: Because an elephant has stood on their ears! Don't you feel any responsibility!? You moulded his mind, Olya. To serve the revolution.

OSIP: All artists 'serve'. Either things as we dream they could be, or things as they are, adding to the dust that settles on all our hopes. Volya was the best of the Futurists. But the Future is receding, by the day. It's over, Lili.

LILI: It will never be over...

OSIP: Everywhere in Moscow bedbugs are crawling out of the mattresses where they've been hiding. Everybody wants to close their doors, substitute Christmas cake for love of the Commune. They're all busy, staking their claims. Soon, the comfortable will feel sorry for the poor, and the poor feel ashamed and inadequate again.

LILI: You go... I intend to stay.

OSIP: I've found work in Odessa, on the Black Sea. Editing the local newspaper.

LILI: You too, staking your little claim?

OSIP: Surviving. There are branches on every branch. Alternatives to every alternative.

LILI: And I'm to come with you...as what? Your wife? We dreamt a different future.

OSIP: I dreamt mass production would create peace and leisure for the masses. It has created only the possibility of mass consumption. The merchants and pilfering bureaucrats are back. Soon salesmanship will be all. And everything sold, every thing consumed, in the petty world of each man's little family room.

LILI: I will not be part of that.

OSIP: Lili, I love Volya as much as you do...

LILI: Then stay! Be here for him. For once in your life do what your heart must tell you is right.

OSIP: I am going to pack, now. You can come, or stay here, as you wish. You're free to choose. Always have been.

Exit OSIP.

Scene Sixteen

TITLE: 'the throat of my very own song'
MAYAKOVSKY steps to the audience. Shirt sleeves.

MAYAKOVSKY: Is there no one out there? Are you all church mice? Except him! You, on the back row. Stop flapping your jaws. Are you a man or a cupboard!? Comrades… Thank you all for coming this evening. I'd particularly like to welcome a very large party from the Politburo. He's sitting over there.

He takes out the slips of paper.

Some questions have been handed to me. A Comrade Filchkin has sent this up. Where are you Filchkin? Ah… Cheer up… Smile. Laugh… I laughed when you came in!! You ask me to remember that, in art, from the sublime to the ridiculous, is but a short step. (*MAYAKOVSKY takes a step backwards.*) You are correct.

Silence.
MAYAKOVSKY chooses another slip of paper.

One from a Proletcult Comrade. (*He sniffs the paper.*) I knew something about me was stinking. You say you think my poetry is unintelligible to the masses. I think if the comrades can't understand my verse, I need to find better Comrades.

Silence.

Twenty years of work!
Agitprop sticks in my teeth.
I'd rather write romance for you
More profit, and more charm
But I subdued myself
Setting my heel
On the throat of my very own song…
Listen Comrades of posterity
To the Agitator, the rabble rouser.

My verse will reach you
Not as an arrow in a Cupid-lyred chase
Not as a worn kopek reaches a coin collector
Not as the light of dead stars reaches you.
My verse will bridge the mountain chain of years
As an aquaduct, by slaves of Rome
Constructed, still brings water to the city.
The years of trial and days of hunger, ordered the likes
    of me
To march under the Red Flag.
We opened volumes of Marx
As we would open the shutters in our own house.
But we did not have to read to make up our minds,
Which side to join, which side to fight on.
I don't give a spit for tons of bronze
I don't give a shit for slimy marble.
My words brought me no roubles to spare
No craftsman has made mahogany chairs for my home.
In all conscience, I need nothing
Except a freshly laundered shirt.
When I appear before the Central Committee
Of the coming bright years
Instead of a Bolshevik party card
I'll raise above the heads of the gang of self seeking
Poets and crooks
All the hundred volumes of my Communist Committed
    books.

Silence.

Thank you for that burst of indifference. That will be all
from me. My throat is wrecked. Frogs have built their
home there. Goodnight sweet chickens. One more brief
poem. One you'll maybe understand.

Broiled chickies
Broiled chickies
Don't you chickens want to live?
How come you are broiled?

How come you are broiled?

MAYAKOVSKY goes.
Music.

Scene Seventeen

TITLE: '1930'
TITLE: 'love's boat has crashed on philistine reefs'
MAYAKOVSKY wrapped in overcoat. Enter LILI.
The music ends.

LILI: How are you?

MAYAKOVSKY: Lonely as the last eye of a man going to join the blind. Maybe they're right, Lili? My words are unintelligible to the masses.

LILI: Annushka learnt your poem about the horse, by heart. 'Don't cry, dear child, We're each a bit of a horse, of course. Everyone's a horse in some sort of way.'

MAYAKOVSKY: Did you know, Catherine the Great, fell while riding. The horse rolled on top of her. The Imperial whore was no more. I'm going to buy Stalin a horse! A bloody, big, heavy cart horse. I saw the new day coming before him, because I was up all night questioning the stars. He should love me for that!

LILI: Others do… I do… (*Pause.*) Remember when we first met? You talked about poetry, without punctuation. No full stops, no separations, one thing flowing into another. Like life, you said. Rhythms, not rules. I have loved and lived my life like that…

MAYAKOVSKY: And it's come to this: you and me, huddled here. The last of the Futurists… The new people of a new life. The reins of the world in our five fingered hands. I don't want a heaven without a heart, Lili. A millennium without love, and no belief in anything.

LILI: You can write. The way you used to. The way you want to.

MAYAKOVSKY: Hide in another 'forest of words'…?

LILI: Go somewhere. Rest. Get back your strength.

MAYAKOVSKY: The summer cottage in Pushkino. Sit and watch the sun dawn and sing in a tattered world. Move along since move we must the sun and me…

LILI: Why not?

MAYAKOVSKY: It is beautiful there…

LILI: We could reach it before sunset…

MAYAKOVSKY:
> Every cow has a nest
> Every camel a child

There's a park, in Petrograd. And in the park, there's a great oak tree. And under the oak tree, there's a Poet's grave. Every new government removes the body put there by its predecessors and installs one of its own. If I used more suitable words, they might bury me there. Or maybe I'll just pass over Russia, like a slanted rain. (*Pause.*) Oh… My throat is raw with bawling…

LILI: I'll get you some tea. Camomile.

MAYAKOVSKY: Camomile… What a pretty word.

LILI kisses him lightly and exits.
MAYAKOVSKY takes out his gun and spins the chamber.

> If only to believe in the hereafter
> So easy. A trial trip.
> It's enough
> To stretch out your hand
> And in an instant
> The bullet
> Will chart

A thundering path to the hereafter.
What can I do if I
Entirely
With all the forces of my heart
I believed in life.
And still
Believe?...

MAYAKOVSKY puts down the gun.

Not a good method. The vote of no confidence.

Let me live out what is mine.
So that love won't be the servant
Of marriages
Lusts
Loaves
Damning the bed
Getting up from couches
To let love march through the universe
So that on the day
When grief ages you
Not to whine and beg in Christ's name,
So that
At the first cry:
– 'Comrade!'
So that
When you shout
– 'Comrade!'
the whole earth will turn toward you
so as not to love
the victim of households
So that from now on
Of your kith and kin
The father would be
At least the whole world
And the earth your mother.

MAYAKOVSKY picks up the gun again.

Now I'm free of love and posters.
The clawed bear of jealousy lies skinned.
As they say, the incident is closed.
Love's boat has crashed on philistine reefs.
You and I are quits, and there is no point
Listing mutual pain, sorrow and hurts.
Look what stillness in the world.
Night has covered the sky in starlit tribute.
At such hours you rise and you speak
To the Ages, history, and the universe.

MAYAKOVSKY puts the gun to his head.

LILI: (*Sings offstage.*)
I'll take my heart
Wrapped in tears of pain
And carry it
Like a dog
Who drags
To his kennel home
A paw run over by a train
Almighty! A pair of hands you invented
Arranged for everyone
A head like this
Why didn't you see to it
That without being in pain tormented
We could
Kiss and kiss and kiss…

FINIS